PRINCIPLES OF
CHILD PSYCHOTHERAPY

PRINCIPLES OF CHILD PSYCHOTHERAPY

By

DONALD J. CAREK, M.D.

Associate Professor of Psychiatry
Acting Chairman, Division of Human Behavior
Medical College of Wisconsin
Child Psychiatrist
Milwaukee Children's Hospital Psychiatry Center
Milwaukee, Wisconsin

CHARLES C THOMAS • PUBLISHER
Springfield • Illinois • U.S.A.

Published and Distributed Throughout the World by
CHARLES C THOMAS • PUBLISHER
BANNERSTONE HOUSE
301–327 East Lawrence Avenue, Springfield, Illinois, U.S.A.
NATCHEZ PLANTATION HOUSE
735 North Atlantic Boulevard, Fort Lauderdale, Florida, U.S.A.

© *1972, by* CHARLES C THOMAS • PUBLISHER
ISBN 0-398-02254-2
Library of Congress Catalog Card Number: 78-165879

With THOMAS BOOKS *careful attention is given to all details of
manufacturing and design. It is the Publisher's desire to present
books that are satisfactory as to their physical qualities and artistic
possibilities and appropriate for their particular use.* THOMAS
BOOKS *will be true to those laws of quality that assure a good name
and good will.*

Printed in the United States of America
CC-11

For Fran, who patiently offers unending encouragement and support to my efforts, and for our children.

PREFACE

Since the development of child psychotherapy as an entity has followed upon the heels of the development of adult psychotherapy, often psychotherapy of children has been discussed primarily in comparison to adult psychotherapy rather than as an entity unto itself. While there is something to be said for the notion that psychotherapy is psychotherapy and the process of psychotherapy remains the same regardless of the patient, there are things peculiar to the child in his development that do make child psychotherapy unique and an entity unto itself. Accordingly, the aim of this book is to outline those principles that ought to guide the child psychotherapist in his approach to the child and his family.

At the risk of being trite, the emphasis in this book has been placed on a reasonable approach that does not fall back on theoretical biases and assumptions, but rather that is based on clinically observable and demonstrable phenomena. The added risk in such an approach is that the reader may be quick to conclude, "Well, of course, it's just a matter of common sense," without appreciating that once again the "mere common sense" is the well-honed skill of the disciplined clinician and not unbridled intuition.

It would also be appropriate for the prospective reader of this book to ask, "What, if anything, new do you have to offer?" What the book has to offer in this regard is an integrated, overall approach to child psychotherapy from initial assessment to termination. In contrast, one is likely to ordinarily find a bit here and another bit there in the literature concerning specific aspects of child psychotherapy without there being a concise integration of the basic principles of child psychotherapy.

Lastly, it perhaps needs to be spelled out clearly that

this is not a book on therapeutic techniques—not a book on "how to do child psychotherapy." Rather, it is hoped that this book might help the child psychotherapist develop more clearly his own framework of guiding principles from which he can derive his own specific approaches to children and families.

Donald J. Carek

ACKNOWLEDGMENTS

Over the several years that this book was in the making, there were a number of people who supported the idea of a book on child psychotherapy, and they were helpful in stimulating the evolution of the final product found in this book.

I feel especially indebted to Dr. Saul Harrison, with whom I originally entertained the idea of writing a book on child psychotherapy even as we co-authored another book. Together we drew up the original outlines for this book, but my move to Milwaukee introduced obstacles that were insurmountable to us even in the best of our intentions. Nonetheless, Dr. Harrison's continued encouragement proved to be an important spark to my ultimate completion of the task we had originally set for ourselves. More importantly, I feel most indebted to Dr. Harrison for his role in the development of this book through his association as teacher and subsequently as colleague and co-author. In all these associations he has done much to help me shape my own ideas on psychotherapy of children.

It was also Dr. H. David Sackin and the entire staff at the Psychiatric Center at Milwaukee Children's Hospital that offered me generous support and encouragement in my endeavors. I am especially grateful to Mrs. Gail Johnson for her critical comments and suggestions about organization of this book.

A word of gratitude is also due to Dr. Lucille Glicklich and Mr. Irv Raffe who critically read the manuscript.

At the same time I feel grateful to Dr. Stuart Finch and my former colleagues at Children's Psychiatric Hospital in Ann Arbor for their invaluable associations that have nurtured my development in child psychotherapy.

Lastly, it was through the secretarial assistance of Mrs. Karen Spindler and Mrs. Karen Shepherd that the manuscripts came to be.

CONTENTS

PRINCIPLES OF
CHILD PSYCHOTHERAPY

I

A CONCEPTUAL MODEL FOR CHILD PSYCHOTHERAPY

SYLVIA BRODY observes that child psychotherapy appears to be a theoretical orphan in contrast to both adult psychotherapy and child analysis that have a parent in classic psychoanalysis. She goes on to note that "the term child psychotherapy includes diverse methods of treatment (interpretive therapy, play therapy, release therapy, guidance, counseling, remedial education and the group therapies) and seems to serve as a loose name for the many forms of treatment of children other than analysis." She states that it is not yet a name for exclusively defined and related therapeutic techniques. "Numberless contributions from psychiatry and allied fields deal with aspects of theory and practice of child psychotherapy; those based upon psychoanalysis are usually the most theoretically complete." Noting that "authors often do not state, nor is it possible to determine, whether the techniques they have used lie more within the psychoanalytic or other theoretical framework," Brody goes on to define child psychotherapy in a way familiar to many in the field. She defines it as "a psychoanalytically-oriented psychotherapy which consists of the alleviation of a specific neurotic symptom or of a specific form of emotional distress, and the reduction of a related anxiety, through interpretation of the most dynamically relevant conscious conflict, in a one-to-one relationship between therapist and child." She then, however, goes on to differentiate it from child psychoanalysis and ends up discussing the technique of child therapy by borrowing guidelines from adult psychotherapy.

3

In this manner Brody does what is so commonly done in child psychotherapy. In the day-to-day interchange—formal and informal—between those working with adults and those working with children, comparisons between child therapy and adult therapy are everyday fare. There are those who firmly insist that the process of therapy in both is the same, while there are those who with equal conviction insist that the two entail different processes. Arguments pro and con center around assertions like the following: "Children are different from adults" or "children are different from adults but engage in therapy similarly." "The work with children is more demanding because the therapist needs to be more active." "It is so difficult to communicate with the child since he can not express himself well."

It appears that those with a more cursory contact with a wide spectrum of children, i.e. if the therapist remains steeped in work with adult patients and/or he has a practice limited to intensive therapy or psychoanalysis, are more inclined to emphasize the similarities between adult and child therapy. Those more actively working with children from a broader base may be more inclined to emphasize the differences. In the latter such emphasis may originate in several ways. It may be the product of smugness of the given moment when the therapist feels heady with success. It may come when successful work is more elusive or at the end of a hard day; some might say that a hard day for a child therapist is a day on which he goes home muttering, 'I've lost every single game of checkers today."

When more formal comparisons are made between the two fields of therapeutic endeavor, there are several different frameworks in which to make these comparisons. In effect, these comparisons between adult therapy and child therapy then become the conceptual model for child psychotherapy.

First, one can start out with the breakdown of the various steps and processes involved in adult therapy and see how work with children shapes up against the adult model. Certainly, this is the most familiar way to conceptualize child therapy. In this regard, comparisons start with assessment of the patient and proceed through the various stages of therapy. There is the matter of the initiation of therapy and the establishment of a contract that lends itself to the development of a therapeutic alliance. There is consideration of the beginning phase, of the middle phase, and of termination (or terminal phase, if and when the process sours). There is the matter of organization of material so as to deal with it in a reasonable manner according to a rational plan in therapy. Manner of communication between the patient and therapist within the context of current reality or within the reality of the transference and countertransference manifestations rounds out the picture. Tacked on are considerations of the therapeutic value of insight and other psychological operations. Within this framework of comparison between adult and child therapy, the notion of parameters in work with children is likely to creep in repeatedly, especially if psychoanalysis is the specific type of therapy under consideration.

There is a second framework for comparisons. One might look primarily to the patient and end up with comparisons between adult and child therapy on the basis of the relative maturity or immaturity of the patient. In this framework the child is seen as realistically more dependent. He is further seen as likely to stress or strain the process of therapy (taking the adult model as the standard) with the relative immaturity of his various personality functions. It may then be stressed that allowances need to be made or parameters need to be introduced because of the level of the child's object relationships, his limited abstractive and verbal abilities, his tendencies for rapid transference development, his libidinal level, and the instability of libidinal organization—these among the host of personality functions that come into play if and when the child engages in a therapeutic relationship.

Third and last, one can compare the two types of therapeutic endeavors by concentrating on the therapist and what he brings into this relationship. Specific factors for consideration include the manner of communication (talk versus play), the need for the therapist to be active or inactive or passive, and the therapist's ability for empathy with the child.

But why the comparison between adult and child therapy as a model for child psychotherapy? Several explanations readily come to mind. Since child therapists ordinarily precipitate or rise from the pool of adult therapists (precipitate or rise depending upon whether one views child therapists as the cream of the crop), child therapy in effect becomes that which the therapist takes with him from adult psychotherapy. As such, it is logical for the therapist to make comparisons between adult and child therapy, as he has a need to maintain a beacon of certainty until he establishes his new identity. Unfortunately, however, much too often the comparison smacks of an apologia, a justification for existence as a legitimate activity or discipline. This sort of attitude is especially noticeable when one hears or reads discussions of child analysis. Is or is not child analysis true analysis?

Though it is understandable that child therapy is and will be compared to adult therapy, to build a conceptual model on such comparisons does have drawbacks. Something about the true nature of child psychotherapy is lost in the process if an attempt is made to understand child therapy and teach it in this light. Many times, to do so is to elude the true nature of child therapy. Much too much child psychotherapy ends up living in the shadows of its parent specialty. It is like adult therapy living in the shadows of psychoanalysis. The result is that the "chip off the old block" is the one most revered. In regard to child therapy, the result is undue premium on those things that are specifically prominent in adult psychotherapy.

A gnawing uneasiness about conceptualization still persists. The fact remains that there is a dearth of literature on the subject. Brody, in her previously cited paper, and Buxbaum, in her commonly known article on child therapy, both note how the literature is replete with discussions of therapy and therapeutic techniques utilized in dealing with a particular child with a specific disorder. However, there is practically nothing in terms of a unified, integrative discussion of child psychotherapy and all that it entails. The literature on child therapy is lopsided. First, therapy of children is overshadowed by literature on child psychoanalysis. Second, the existent literature leans toward establishing more securely a premium on intensive therapy which is akin to child analysis. There is a need for delineation of a broader view of child therapy and all that it entails.

While it is easy to expound the need for a broader definition of child therapy and a fuller discussion of all that this work entails, there is no denying as to how there are limitations and even pitfalls in such a definition and discussion. While there is a need for a cohesive, unified framework in which to understand therapeutic material and in which to formulate therapeutic strategy, there is the danger of coming up with something so broad that it becomes meaningless. As such, child therapy would then no longer be a definable, teachable discipline but would involve a process in which each is doing his own thing.

Unfettered of limitations inherent in adult-child therapy comparisons, hopefully child therapists might become less obsessed with worrying about the parameters to be used in child therapy. Hopefully they then might get more to the business of considering the whole process of child psychotherapy in its own light. Looked at in another way—in a developmental fashion—the child therapists need to let the identifications with adult therapy give way to establishment of an identity in child psychotherapeutic work.

In order to establish a conceptual model for child psychotherapy, there are a number of factors specific to the child and the therapy of this child that need to be taken into consideration. I would like to highlight them at this point. The aim here is not to come up with a definitive model for child psychotherapy but to list, question, and discuss those factors from which the foundations of child therapy are established. First, there is the question, Which child is in need of therapy? How much is the decision made on the basis of the child's needs as determined through diagnostic assessment? How much does the decision rest on the assessed or assumed motivation of the child and/or parent? How much does race, socioeconomic level, or financial ability weigh heavily on the decision to recommend and institute therapy? It seems safe to say that in our current state of knowledge there is a denigration of the whole process of assessment and therapy by those who routinely view childhood problems in global terms and see therapy merely in terms of total personality overhauling. Such a view is especially unrealistic because it ignores the process of childhood development.

Anna Freud (1945) has stated that "the decision as to whether a child needs therapeutic help or not can be based on the state of the libidinal development. An infantile neurosis can be treated as a transistory disorder as long as the libido organization of the child remains fluid and shows progressive tendencies. When the libido constellations become rigid, stabilized and monotonous in their expressions, the neurosis is in danger of remaining permanently. This means that treatment is indicated." From here she goes on to note how the evaluator needs to be as intimately familiar with the normal sequence of child development as he is with the neurotic or psychotic disturbance of it. "He is actually faced with the task of judging the normality of the developmental process itself."

So the developmental yardstick is the chief guideline or gauge by which need for therapy is determined. In effect, the child therapist regularly needs to make his assessments in the murky interface between psychopathology and "developmental deviation." Obviously, drawing fine lines is well-nigh impossible, but fortunately the decision for or against therapy does not rest on such fine lines. Call it psychopathological or a developmental deviation, the decision for or against therapy requires additional considerations or even additional time. In effect, the decision rests on demonstration of continued development and evidence of further potential for growth.

A number of things need to be kept in mind about developmental considerations. To weigh the child's overall functioning against developmental expectations does give some objective basis by which to proceed in assessment and arrival at therapeutic determinations. Such an assessment, however, entails a number of subjective elements that can lead to dubious conclusions. First, the assessor needs to guard against rigid expectations of what a child is to do at a particular stage in his development. He must always take into account the individuality of a specific child. Second, he must not become victim of a pessimistic attitude that ignores a child's developmental flexibility. That it is crucial to develop a specific personality function at a specific phase of development is an attractive hypothesis that becomes even more cogent if veiled allusions are made to the laws of imprinting originally described by Hess in goslings.

At times it may need to be emphasized that existence of such laws of imprinting in human development has never been demonstrated. It did appear as though Spitz's studies in development of institutionalized infants pointed in that direction. However, his investigative approach has been questioned. Furthermore, as Bettelheim notes, experience in the kibbutzim pretty much negates the notion of an invariably deleterious effect from multiple mothering. Rather the quality of constancy, be it in a person or in an institution, may be the important factor. Clinical reports also point in other directions. For example, Beres has reported on the more adequate than anticipated adaptation of adolescents who suffered severe deprivation in early childhood.

Assessment of a child's development almost invariably presses one to make fine distinctions between what is stressful and what is traumatic in a child's experiences. The most common error is to gear history taking so as to catalogue the stresses to which a child was exposed rather than to gain an understanding of when and how the child's stress proved to be traumatic for this child. In effect, unwittingly, the stress and the trauma become identified. Because the child has a history of a particular stress—early maternal loss, serious illness, or injury—he is assumed to have been traumatized by these events. Attention is directed toward what the child has faced instead of how he has dealt with the stress. To proceed in this manner is very tempting at times, as it may be infinitely easier to document events than to document experiences. To proceed in this manner may also cause one to lose the richness of individual coping mechanisms that have been so well described by Murphy in her observations of a group of children studied up into adolescence.

Apart from the limitations introduced by the subjectivity of the assessor, current developmental guidelines of themselves are inclined to be distorted because of our incomplete knowledge. The emphasis is likely to be on assessment of psychological functioning, as it is in this area that we have codified guidelines such as Anna Freud's (1965) developmental lines. She in effect directs the examiner to proceed by taking into account integrative personality functioning as it develops around certain personality tasks. It still remains for someone to integrate psychological assessment with the assessment of various biological capacities so as to have a fuller and perhaps an even more realistic understanding of children.

Where do we stand in assessment of biological, physiological, or neurophysiological substrata of psychological functioning? There are Wolff's observations of newborns, i.e., the rhythmicity and patterns of central nervous system discharge which characterize a specific child. There are Fries's observations of different reactive patterns found in newborns. We have Lipton's studies on child-specific differences in autonomic responses of newborns. The point is that there are observations of individual biological variations in children which we still do not understand so as to utilize them in our assessments. However, it would appear that the child therapist will eventually need to integrate such data into his understanding of the psychological functioning of children. It is such integration that will lead to more realistic guidelines by which to assess a particular child's development, make predictions, and arrive at more objective indications for therapy. At this stage of knowledge, the psychoanalytic theory of personality does offer a systematic conceptualization of personality that is necessary in psychotherapy. While it does fill a need, we cannot dismiss comments such as Nuffield makes in regard to theories about personality development. He notes that "at this point it is difficult to have available a systematic theory which can be made operational and which lends itself to the construction of testable hypotheses. Until this can be found, the child psychiatrist builds, to some extent, on quicksand." Furthermore, in our current assessment of children for psychotherapy, there is a danger of establishing too rigid a hierarchy of behavior and personality functioning, which detracts from looking on any individual child as a legitimate variant of the human species that is not epitomized in any one particular life style.

A word of caution is in order since some may look on such comments as nihilistic as they feel reasonably secure in their theoretical stance and since others may use such comments to further nihilistic causes. I do not advocate that we discard our current theories. Rather the plea is for an open-mindedness that acknowledges that our theories are incomplete and that allows us to assimilate new knowledge. While such a plea may sound trite and vacuously pedantic, the fact is that psychotherapists in their zeal can become rigidly dogmatic about their theories so as to act as though they were espousing a religion.

A conceptual model for child psychotherapy also needs to take into account that the bulk of child therapy is crisis intervention in the true sense of the word. Harkening back to earlier comments, the concept of coping and the concept of crisis intervention go hand in hand. Within this context the child is viewed as dealing with one developmental task after another. A crisis arises especially when the process of coping is unduly strained, so that attempts at successful mastery are jeopardized. Determination needs to be made as to why the task is so arduous at the moment. Is it the nature of the

stress or is it in the manner of coping attempts? Is there a lack
of the usual environmental supports upon which the child ordinarily relies? If so, it may be necessary to decide whether
the parents need aid so that they might help their child more
effectively. They might need advice or they may need to see
how they are unwittingly involved in development of the
child's conflicts at the moment. In another instance the therapist bolsters the usual environmental supports by momentarily lending another understanding ear to the child.

Or is it the child himself who is in need of therapeutic intervention? It may be a matter of conflict over specific self-expression at the moment. As such, assistance in the resolution
of current conflicts is in order. Therapeutically this would
be accomplished by helping the child develop awareness—
for example, delineation of conflict and conflictual forces—
and by offering him support in resolution of these conflicts.
Or it may be that the present situation resurrects old conflicts that interfere with current coping attempts. The aim
then might be to enhance the usual reparative process that
proceeds somewhat in this fashion. At this moment in a con-
densed fashion, the child in effect stages, dramatizes, and
in the process resolves an emotional problem that has been
plaguing him since earlier days. In contrast to his previous
functioning, he then is able to function more age-appropri-
ately and without the impediments imposed by these earlier
conflicts. It seems that such crisis-type situations are a
natural way of getting rid of dead weight. What comes to
mind are the variety of school-refusal problems which occur
either when the child with unresolved conflicts over separation from mother first begins school or as he enters puberty
when problems of separation from family again come to the
fore.

An example follows:

Ken was an eleven-year-old boy who did not return to school
after Christmas recess because of severe right-sided headaches
and associated photophobia. After he had been home from
school two weeks with these symptoms, he was admitted to the
hospital for evaluation. Diagnostic examinations shed little light

on the picture and he was discharged from the hospital with a a diagnosis of migraine headache. It was at the time of discharge that psychiatric consultation was requested because Ken made a fuss about leaving the hospital. He again complained of severe headache and photophobia and he insisted that he could not go home. In effect, he developed a "home-refusal syndrome."

It was then learned that Ken had become very much distraught at the end of the previous December upon return home from another city where the family had attended the wedding of Ken's older brother. Ken cried and lamented that his brother would never again return home to live with the family. His subsequent headaches were now felt to be part of a school-refusal syndrome precipitated by his brother's marriage.

After much time was spent dealing with Ken in his concerns about discharge from the hospital, he did get home the same day though his father ended up carrying him from the car into the home. Follow-up was arranged and it was decided that Ken would return to school on Monday. It turned out that Ken did return to school on Monday but only with firm parental persistence that fell just short of physical coercion.

Ken adopted an extremely regressed position over the weekend prior to his return to school and upon his return from school daily that first week-and-a-half. He cried a great deal and complained about how miserable he felt. He insisted that he be returned to the hospital as he claimed that he would go crazy if he were forced to remain at home. He made repeated phone calls at all hours of the day and evening to his psychiatrist and his pediatrician to plaintively and in a most infantile, whining manner plead his case to return to the hospital. He ordinarily prefaced and punctuated his comments with "Doctor, I feel so frustrated." Resisting the temptation to share with Ken his own intense feelings of frustration, his psychiatrist in effect told him that better days were ahead and further frustrated him as he told him things could be worse. On the phone and in several therapy sessions he confronted Ken with his observations that Ken's behavior reflected a wish to remain a little boy who would not have to grow up. He repeatedly reminded Ken that he had a need to fall into this this position because of the fear generated in him by his brother's marriage. It was interpreted to him that in his behavior he seemed to indicate that if he remained the sick little helpless boy, he would not need to worry about growing up to marry and leave home like his brother.

After a week-and-a-half that was extremely trying for all the family, Ken returned to his original level of functioning, i.e. he again became asymptomatic. He terminated his contacts with the psychiatrist by cancelling his last appointment with the explanation that he would be busy in a basketball game at the time of his scheduled appointment.

Such acting out of a conflict in an acute crisis-type manner is not restricted to the school-refusal syndrome, as the following example illustrates:

Kathy, a fifteen-year-old girl, was referred for psychiatric consultation the day after she impulsively made a suicide gesture with ingestion of aspirin. This impulsive action was most unusual for Kathy, as she ordinarily was inclined to be studied in her behavior. Briefly, history and examination pointed toward an insecure young lady who was inclined toward intermittent, brief periods of depression that were not disruptive of her generally adequate functioning. Kathy was embarrassed about her suicide attempt and was insistent that there would never be a repeat performance.

It was striking that Kathy began to sob uncontrollably when she mentioned that her father had died when she was two years old. She was puzzled by her tears, since she had no recollection of his death. She did recall, however, that recently she had been thinking a great deal about her dead father and had wished that they were together. In the subsequent two sessions Kathy showed no similar emotion. Rather she was embarrassed and puzzled that she should have cried when she originally talked about her father's death. Finally, the therapist suggested to Kathy that there appeared to be some connection between her recent thoughts about her father and her suicide attempt. He prefaced these interpretive remarks with the observation that her tears had pointed to unresolved but repressed feelings about her father and his death. Kathy gave a start when he further observed that her attempt at suicide appeared to reflect a wish to be reunited with her father. After a pause, she simply added soberly that somehow this made sense to her.

PARENTAL INVOLVEMENT

A conceptual model for child psychotherapy needs to take into account parental involvement in such therapy. There are two extreme positions that can be taken, each of which can be supported theoretically. There are those who routinely demand no parental involvement except maybe to chauffeur the child to sessions and definitely to sign the monthly payment check to underwrite the whole process. Those who take this stand emphasize the child's remarkably early development of a relatively independent personality structure with internalized conflicts. At the other extreme are those who routinely see the parents to be significantly disturbed and in need of therapy for themselves, either individually or conjointly. Those who take this stand emphasize the "facilitating" or "nonfacilitating" environment in normal and pathological development. It is interesting, however, that therapists in private practice are likely to take the former stand while clinic staff members are likely to emphasize a need to have both child and parents involved in therapy routinely. While each group can support its stand theoretically, each may err by going from theory to the case at hand rather than beginning with the needs of this particular child in this particular family. As a general rule, it does seem wise to keep the whole process of therapy child-centered unless specifically contraindicated. There are a variety of clichés that can burden us in our work and can direct our glance in one direction or another. For example, the idea of "emissary patient" may direct our glance away from the problem at hand as we get accustomed to thinking of more general considerations. One can develop an unrealistic set in which he routinely sees parents as coming for help for themselves rather than for their children. Looking for other problems can also be part of a tendency to proceed cynically with the attitude that the only reality is the hidden reality.

It may be helpful at this point just to highlight a number of factors a therapist needs to keep in mind as he deals with parents. He needs first to appreciate that even if the child's specific problems are symptomatic of more general or family problems, the only way to these more general problems may be through dealing with the child's specific problems. To tell the parents that they are the problem may fail on several counts. There are those parents who invite such "attack" or "condemnation." In turn they may prove to be in search of an assuagement of their guilt rather than in search for understanding that can lead to resolution of the problems at hand. Or the therapist's comments may fall on deaf ears either because they make no sense to the family or because the family feels insulted.

If the parents are actually involved intimately in their child's difficulties at the moment through their own conflicts, it may be necessary to help the parents become more meaningfully aware of this fact. They may become more motivated to seek help for themselves if, for example, they are given an opportunity to prove to themselves that they do have certain problems. Such awareness may come from an experience of helplessness in trying to carry out what the doctor prescribed, be it trying to tune in on the child's behavior or trying to respond to him in a more reasonable fashion. There is the danger that the therapist may approach the parents as hopelessly inflexible and as incapable of responding to anything short of therapy geared toward their total personal reorganization. Or there is the tendency to assess parents to be good parents or bad parents. Apart from the fact that such diagnoses are ordinarily meaningless, it is worthwhile to harken to Casuso's (Panel Report, 1965) observation that "if we could accept that non-traumatic parents are not of this earth, we could be more objective in enlisting their help when needed."

Distinctions between past and current levels of parental functioning also need to be made. The parent or parents may have been intimately involved in the development of specific neurotic distortions in a child because of some stresses at a previous time in the family's history—the depression of mother during the early critical years of the child's life, illness, death, financial struggles that exerted stresses and strains in family interaction. However, the parents currently may be able to function at a reasonable level. Or it may be forgotten that a parent who is reasonable in one area of functioning may have difficulty dealing reasonably with his child in regards to particular impulse expressions because of his own specific unresolved conflicts. He may have no problems when it comes to approaching his child regarding other matters, however. A clinical example comes to mind.

> Mr. K. brought his son Tom for psychiatric consultation after Tom and a friend played with matches that led to an attic fire which could have been disastrous. When Tom had played with matches several times previously, his parents felt they had reprimanded him sternly on each occasion. However, when it came to the specifics of how the parents dealt with Tom on these occasions, the father volunteered that he regularly had found himself uneasy in dealing with the fire setting. Whereas he generally felt comfortable in disciplining and punishing Tom, it was different when he had to deal with Tom's fire setting. At these times the father felt paralyzed. He found himself feeling that he did not know what to do, primarily because he felt afraid that anything he did might end up being the wrong thing to do.
>
> It struck the therapist that Mr. K. was generally reasonable and effective in his discipline and it appeared that his overall appraisal of his child's behavior was realistic. The therapist therefore thought it would be desirable to "shore up" the father in this area of his unresolved conflicts which were being mobilized by the son's fire setting. In effect, he counselled the father to treat the fire setting as misbehavior rather than sick behavior and deal with Tom accordingly. The therapist in effect was hoping to have the father fall back on the authority of the therapist for support in ego and superego functioning if and when he might falter rather than react decisively in response to Tom's fire setting.

There may also be the tendency to jump prematurely to the conclusion that a child's problems are a result of the parent's pathological functioning. Sandler wisely notes that "it is not enough to accept at face value the proposition that a disturbed mother will create a disturbed child. We ought to know how the disturbance in the mother modifies the child's character development and at the same time we should not underestimate the importance of endopsychic factors in this process."

ENVIRONMENTAL MANIPULATION

Whereas psychotherapy for a parent or for both parents geared toward resolution of their own intrapsychic conflicts may be indicated in specific situations, there is the danger that a child psychotherapist may lean too heavily on this mode of helping parents. Herein the mystique of therapy may shine forth. Therapists unwittingly may attach a certain aura to therapy, especially "intensive, long-term therapy." As a result, it may too quickly become the treatment of choice, while other more conservative and perhaps more specifically indicated forms of environmental manipulation are overlooked.

To talk of environmental manipulation is many times to run the risk of being accused of using dirty words. Joselyn has noted that to acknowledge the effectiveness of environmental manipulation in properly selected cases has one stand a chance of being confronted with the supercilious comment of his more erudite colleagues that the core conflict was not treated. Joselyn makes a very important point that may be neglected in psychotherapy of children. If parents are involved in therapy, they "will not change quickly, especially since often the parents' therapy will be oriented to the parents' neuroses, not to the immediate needs of the child; the parent's therapist will not give much guidance to those parents and often would consider it interference if the child's therapist intervened very frequently."

Unfortunately, much too often such is the therapy plan and such is the progress of therapy when therapeutic responsibility for a family is split among several therapists. It ends up that nobody does help the family deal with current, pressing realities out of fear that such intervention may interfere with therapy. In such an arrangement the therapist is unduly optimistic at best if he anticipates meaningful results in a reasonable period of time, i.e., changes in the parents that will lead them to be more positively effective with their child at his current level of development. With the usual intensive, nondirective therapy, perhaps these parents will develop valuable insights about themselves and will change in time to deal more realistically with their grandchildren who will be feeling the pinch of being raised by persistently neurotic parents whose therapists believe that the way to a child's problems is through the complicated maze of his parents' unconscious!

Negative feelings about environmental manipulation breed on another prejudice that may be found among child psychotherapists. An undue premium may be placed on autoplastic adaptation over alloplastic adaptation as though the latter were always on the pathological side. There is a danger of being so inflexible so as to emphasize to an unreasonable and even unrealistic extent the need for resolution of intrapsychic conflict or the need for personality change rather than look for possible environmental readjustments. "You will just carry the problems with you" may be a catchy phrase but may not be all that accurate.

It might be argued that as soon as the therapist works at all with the parents in conjunction with the child's psychotherapy, he is engaging in environmental manipulation; be it giving them advice or getting the parents involved in psychotherapy for themselves with the child's psychotherapist or with another therapist, the aim is to bring about some change in them that will be conducive to the child's development or corrective of some interaction that is felt to distort his development. As such, the giving of advice or the psychotherapy entails environmental manipulation, the former being a more overt or more direct form while the latter may be more clandestine or more indirect. Unfortunately, environmental manipulation carries negative connotations primarily because it may be considered in very simplistic terms. The stereotype may be that of the authoritative physician or therapist pontificating to the parents as to what they should do to or for the child. "Let's try this and if it doesn't work we'll see what else we might come up with." Furthermore, such dicta may entail little thought other then a cursory assessment of the problem at hand.

In contrast, a more meaningful type of environmental manipulation would seem to entail more deliberative assessment and conceptualization. Nor need it rest on an authoritative stance on the part of the therapist; rather it can, and I would say it should, rest on the usual psychotherapeutic principles, if psychotherapy is denoted as follows:

1. A psychological means of helping people, with the emphasis specifically on development of awareness.
2. A process which is based on a systematized understanding of people and their functioning.
3. A process in which the underlying theories are accessible to critical scrutiny.
4. A process in which the therapist in one way or another informs the patient about the process so as to help him be party to the transactions.

PROCESS OF PSYCHOTHERAPY

In order to develop a conceptual model for psychotherapy of children, one needs to consider various features of the therapeutic process. There is the need to look at how the child and therapist participate in this process. Throughout these considerations an eye needs to be kept on how therapy works.

How is the therapist to approach the child in psychotherapy? What role does the therapist assume? To answer it simply, it might be said that the therapist needs to consider whether or to what extent he will be a "real" person to the child, in contrast to a "transference" figure. But further consideration needs to be given to what goes into being a "real" person to the child in therapy. No one would question that the therapist needs to be a truly human person in whom the child can sense warmth and understanding. To be real in this sense needs to be differentiated from being real in terms of responding to the neurotically determined transference expectation of the child. There is a danger that in his attempts to be a "real" person, the therapist may not discriminate between these different approaches. In the delineation of roles the therapist needs to differentiate between the educator and the therapist, even while he appreciates that in psychotherapy with children the distinction between education and therapy tends to be fuzzy. In fact, there is a great deal of education that goes into much of the therapeutic work with children.

There is the matter of educating the child about therapy itself. One might argue that the bulk of education in therapy centers around education of the child about the therapeutic process itself. Yet the therapist in treating a child is dealing with a naturally curious being of whom it may be unrealistic to expect that he suspend his curiosity. The child therapist does need always to differentiate for himself, for example, how much of the child's quest for information reflects natural childhood curiosity and how much curiosity is used in the service of resistance. When to merely analyze and when to satisfy the child's curiosity? Ordinarily, it is helpful for purposes of conceptual clarity to think in terms of therapy beginning where education fails, and education beginning or resuming at the point where therapy ends. Educative endeavors ordinarily will be of the reeducative variety, primarily in the context of dealing with the child's neurotic distortions of previous educative material. Put another way, it is helpful to think that a therapist needs to concentrate primarily on expanding the child's total awareness and on the resolution of intrapsychic conflicts so that he may be responsive to his daily educative experiences.

THERAPEUTIC ALLIANCE

The nature of a therapeutic alliance with the child also needs to be weighed. It cannot be underestimated how much the fact that the child is brought by another—by a parent and so frequently against his will—may have an impact on the development of a therapeutic relationship. Some children acknowledge a need for assistance and get involved in therapy accordingly. When the going is rough, others fall back on "but I did not want to be here in the first place and I

am here only because my mother forces me to come." In
the face of such protests, a child may still become very much
involved in the whole process. Others protest and do nothing
but sit back and fight the whole process, as they never become convinced of the need for therapy or never become
convinced that therapy may satisfy their needs.

When and how does the child engage in a "therapeutic
alliance" or "working alliance" with the therapist? These
terms are used to designate, in Greenson's terms, "the relatively nonneurotic, rational rapport which the patient has
with his analyst." He goes on to note that "working alliance"
stresses the vital element of this aspect of the therapeutic
alliance, i.e. "the patient's capacity to work purposefully in
the treatment situation." This facet of the therapeutic relationship may be especially difficult to establish with the
child, as it may be much easier for him to view the therapist
as friend or foe than as a relatively more neutral "participant
observer." While it is true that therapy needs to be primarily an experience and not an explanation, it is the "observing
something together" and "seeing something together" that
makes the therapeutic experience unique.

The degree of the therapist's activity also becomes a special consideration in child psychotherapy. This activity cov-
ers a whole range of possible maneuvers. It ranges from
directive participation in sessions with children—asking
questions, having the child concentrate on some particular
material, suggesting that the child engage in some particular play—to stepping in if necessary to physically restrain
the uncontrolled, assaultive child. In a panel discussion on
child analysis, one analyst recommended that the child analyst stay in one spot while with the child. The other recommended his moving about in the office. The point they raise
is a valid one that each therapist needs to consider. Neither
was arbitrary in his proposal but essentially discussed the
possible impact of the therapist's physical activity or in-
activity on the therapeutic relationship. Yet with certain
children coming to therapy, the therapist has no choice but

to move around. In fact, he may need to restrain the child if he himself hopes to remain intact, and if he is to keep the premises in one piece. However, the need for action is not always so clear-cut. If the child has established at least a semblance of a positive relationship, it may be possible to help him control himself by ending a session prematurely if and when he becomes destructive or physically assaultive. Another situation prevails when a child wanted out yesterday and is destructive. It would seem that as a therapist becomes more skilled, he probably needs to intervene less and less in a physical manner. Or it could also be that experience guides a therapist to be selective in his choice of patients so that he avoids "getting stuck" with the physically assaultive.

PLAY IN THERAPY

While it is generally accepted that play is a manner of expression and communication in psychotherapy, there is need to determine when and how to utilize the child's play in therapy. The aim here is merely to raise some points about play therapy that might be taken into account in general considerations of a conceptual model for child psychotherapy. Some might emphasize the ventilative aspects; others might quickly get at the symbolic elements and deal with such features of play. Others might simply concentrate on the type of play chosen. Some utilize board games such as checkers or Sorry, while others outlaw such games from the start. When is play just an enjoyable activity with which to avoid boredom or contain anxiety and when is it a useful vehicle in therapy?

HOW PSYCHOTHERAPY WORKS

A conceptual model for child psychotherapy needs also to consider the factors operative in therapeutic effectiveness. How does psychotherapy work? Some may concentrate on one factor, such as Frank, who concludes that all psychotherapy is based on persuasion or suggestion. Others might emphasize the importance of insight and see

any other goal or achievement in therapy to be inferior.
Yet it seems safe to say that most would agree that there
is no one factor by which to explain therapeutic effectiveness. Rather there are a number of factors that bear
an impact to varying degrees in various patients. Foremost
in any such consideration needs to be the relationship itself.
Joselyn notes that in certain cases the results of psychotherapy are surprisingly successful even while there is no
clear reason to account for this success. She further observes
that success in such cases appears to result from the stimulation provided by the child's quick response to the interpersonal
relationship with the therapist. The following clinical example, which probably strikes a chord in most child therapists,
illustrates this point.

> Joe was a ten-year-old boy who was brought for therapy
> primarily because of his academic underachievement and
> social isolation at school and at home. In therapy he was
> generally found to be a quiet, passive, but obstinate youngster
> who ended up saying practically nothing during the six months
> he was seen in therapy. If the therapist suggested they play
> a board or card game, Joe would usually express an interest.
> On rare occasions he himself would ask the therapist to play
> such a game, and on even rarer occasions he brought along a
> game from home. As time went on, Joe said nothing and did
> nothing but sit impassively. About the only thing he did ac-
> knowledge was the fact that he did not want to be in therapy,
> as he saw no need to be there.
>
> Finally, the therapist decided they were going nowhere
> fast, and he saw no reason to expect further developments
> if he continued seeing Joe. He therefore made arrangements to
> see Joe's mother with the idea of explaining to her that it
> would be wise to terminate at this point. He planned to tell
> her that if further intervention appeared necessary, some type
> of placement outside the home might be considered.
>
> The therapist never did get to paint a rather bleak picture
> for the mother, because she reported how impressed she was
> with Joe's progress. She summed up her comments by saying
> that she thought that Joe had at the moment gone as far as
> he could with his therapist. While on the surface this might
> sound like a backhanded compliment, she actually did go on
> to cite the evidence of Joe's improved functioning and seemed

realistic in portraying him as having arrived at a plateau. The fact is that he was more assertive at home, and he was showing progress socially and academically at school.

Joselyn goes on to question the use of professional time for this type of readily instituted "relationship therapy." She raises a point well worth serious consideration when she concludes that such therapy might be carried out more effectively in a child's environment by a sensitive and intuitive person who was alerted to the needs of the child and who was offered some guidance in meeting those needs. The fact is that the relationship itself does seem to be the prime healing force in so much of child therapy. The gnawing question repeatedly arises as to how long to continue therapy on this basis if the relationship alone appears to be the therapeutic factor. First, the therapist needs to remember that his relationship with the patient is one that may be difficult to duplicate with a nonprofessional. The fact that he is viewed as "healer," stamped so by society, does give him leverage (some might call it "magic") that might not readily be attained by one not so endowed by society. Though appropriate use of already limited manpower may prompt other arrangements when relationship therapy alone seems to be in the offing, appreciation of the process of therapy will forestall hasty changes in treatment plans. The fact is that many times a child may initially proceed for months in therapy talking about everything but yet nothing and playing games endlessly before he finally settles into more than relationship therapy. Intertwined with the benefits that accrue from the relationship are the benefits derived from psychotherapy as a "corrective emotional experience." This factor also appears to be an integral part of so much child therapy. Being accepted as a person worthy of being taken seriously, being allowed to experience a wide range of emotions without criticism, and being afforded a greater opportunity to express himself more freely all lend themselves to making the therapy a corrective emotional exprience. It becomes such an experience more or less to the extent that the child's previous or outside therapy experiences were quite the opposite.

Akin to "corrective emotional experience" is catharsis or abreaction, whose value also needs to be considered in child psychotherapy. If one uses catharsis in a broad sense, i.e. ventilation of emotion or pent-up affect not necessarily related to a specific traumatic event, then it is seen to be a major factor in therapeutic effectiveness. Its need is highlighted by the fact that a child repeatedly needs to deal with crises or experiences that lend themselves to pent-up emotion. To the extent that he copes with this affect ineffectively he may fall back on various maladaptive ways that are reflected in developmental distortions. Reversal of the process will necessitate mobilization of affect and a certain degree of catharsis. The value of abreaction or catharsis many times seems to be maligned. While to establish it as an endpoint in psychotherapy may be questionable, it is not at all realistic to deny it any role. Perhaps it may be helpful to view catharsis as an intermediate point toward which one strives with many children but which may become an endpoint once it is reached. The ultimate goal ordinarily would be to help the patient move from catharsis to development of modes other than repressive forces to deal with his emotions.

How vital is insight in therapeutic success? While some might consider such a statement iconoclastic, it would seem safe to say that in the bulk of child psychotherapy, development of insight is but frosting on the cake. But disaagreement about the value of insight may revolve around definition of terms. The sort of insight that I am deemphasizing is that which Singer describes as "a rational appreciation of one's behavior and its motivational mainsprings." In contrast, much as Singer does, it would seem more reasonable to put the emphasis in therapy on awareness rather than on understanding, "the awareness of inner situations (and outer situations) which have been dissociated in an attempt to deny them." To some, such awareness may approximate or even be synonymous with insight.

From a very practical standpoint a word of caution about imparting insights to children is in order, as a child's productions often lend themselves so readily to interpretation along libidinal lines if one is so inclined. Sylvester cites an example of a young therapist with a five-year-old. In one session the child lashed together the various chairs in the room, covered the top with masses of paper and crawled in and out of the small openings. When the therapist reported that this behavior was flavored with all sorts of birth fantasy material, the supervisor reminded the therapist that the family had just been away on vacation, and as it turned out, on a camping trip. As the hour was then reviewed, the birth fantasies became hierarchically less significant, and the tent the family used on vacation became a far more likely explanation for the new kind of play. To make an interpretation to the patient along the former line would invite intellectual insights that one could expect to be therapeutically ineffectual.

While it is difficult to say with certainty what accounts for effectiveness in the therapy of any particular child, we do have some understanding of and some control over the various factors involved. As such, it is reasonable to establish a hierarchy of these factors, each of which can become a goal in itself or can lead to a goal. Is there or can there be one specific goal for psychotherapy? The premium in psychotherapy would seem to have to be on development of awareness which is not viewed as a panacea but as an aid for a child to cope more effectively. One would reasonably say that those involved in helping a child develop adequately will need to think in terms of helping a child remain or become accessible to his internal forces and to those environmental forces that ordinarily enhance his personality development. While there are a number of ways in which to help a child heighten this accessibility— and psychotherapy is but one of many—psychotherapy ought to and does have its own unique way to help a child in this regard. While a therapist has a variety of options available to him in his own work, he ought to exercise these therapeutic options within the context of helping the child and family increase their ability to develop ever more awareness.

It is an awareness which is less and less impeded by neurotic constrictions and distortions that lead to maladaptive behavior of one sort or another. It is an awareness that is approached in psychotherapy through an interpersonal relationship in which the striving for such awareness is fostered and in which this aid to fuller development is taught if this skill has not been acquired. However, the therapeutic process needs to be one in which self-reflection with a quest for greater self-awareness is not pursued as an end in itself so that it becomes an obsessive preoccupation with oneself. Rather, as Whyte notes in "The Unconscious Before Freud,"

> The biological "function," in a generalized sense, of this awareness was to assist man in eliminating the clash by modifying either the environment or the activities of the person and thus remove the conditions which evoked the moment of self-awareness. The clear awareness of a distinction of self and environment tended to facilitate adequate delayed responses which would lessen the clash and hence to relax the self-awareness. Thus, *self-awareness is basically self-eliminating;* its biological function is apparently to catalyze processes which tend to remove its cause, in each situation. Consciousness is like a fever which, if not excessive, hastens curative processes, and so eliminates its source. Contrasted with the growth of a plant or an animal, persisting self-awareness is like an illness which continually provokes its own cure, and in the long run usually does so.

While the adult may be in need of insight, i.e. a rational appreciation of his behavior and its motivational mainsprings, the child seems more in need of sharpening his skills to expand his awareness from which might naturally flow insights during the course of his developmental experiences. Put in another way, it seems more important to help a child develop an ever greater awareness of *what* he is doing than that he understand *why*. It would seem that if he can keep his awareness openly available, insight follows as development proceeds. I wonder if we are being especially helpful to a child if we concentrate on the *why* for his motivation. To do so might be to unwittingly foster constrictive rationalizations, as not enough credit is given to the fact that the *why* constitutes a broad base composed of a variety of motivations.

TERMINATION

In the consideration of termination in child psychotherapy, the following clinical anecdote may help to draw attention to an important point.

John was a fourteen-year-old boy who had been referred for psychiatric evaluation because of his mother's concern over his tendency to have "highs and lows" which she felt exceeded the usual adolescent's range. In his low periods he was expressing much pessimism over his future and regularly ended up in heated disagreements with his mother and stepfather.

Though initially anxious about seeing a psychiatrist and in his anxiety denying a need to see one, John soon got to acknowledge that he did have some very unpleasant moments and did have many things on his mind. In the second session he was expressing an interest to become involved in outpatient psychotherapy. At that time John came through as an anxious, depressed adolescent who appeared to be struggling with a great deal of neurotic turmoil. At the same time he appeared to be a very bright and articulate youngster who evidenced considerable introspective ability. It was arranged that John's psychotherapy schedule involve two visits per week and the length of it was undefined. John did keep this schedule faithfully and he remained in therapy for a total of six months.

In the early phase of therapy John was primarily concerned about who was in control of him. At home he saw his mother as trying to control him. In turn he saw himself as controlling her by saying what she liked to hear. In therapy sessions he repeatedly accused the therapist of trying to control him. As therapy proceeded he did get to see how he was extremely busy there doing that which he feared would be done to him, namely, trying to control.

After a couple of months of therapy John began to report

that something had happened to him. He claimed that his
sensitivity had decreased and now he was worried that he might
become quite a "blah" character. Specifically, he noticed that
he was not reacting to "crises" at home as he had previously.
In turn he and his therapist got to review how John had
enjoyed crises at home and had had a need for them that led
to his provoking many a crisis.

By the fifth month of therapy John spontaneously talked of
how it appeared to him that viewing his relationships with
people in terms of who was controlling whom did not seem
realistic. He just did not find himself worrying about who was
in control. However, in therapy he more and more expressed
concern over what his therapist had "done to him." He went
on to observe how nothing seemed to "happen" in any one
particular session, but over the course of the therapy something
had been happening so that he was feeling and acting differently
than before he started his psychotherapy. John acknowledged
that as he felt that the therapist had done something to him
already, he feared what the therapist might do to him if he
remained in therapy. Specifically he feared that he might become completely submissive, a "blah."

In turn the therapist reminded John of his concerns about
who controls whom. Now John acknowledged that there was
something appealing about the idea of becoming passive and submissive with people, such as with his mother. He added that
becoming so seemed to be an easy way to live. Though the
therapist dealt with John's neurotic fears about what might
happen to him in his relationship to his therapist, he agreed
with John's decision to terminate therapy at this point.

The therapist agreed to terminate the psychotherapy of
this youngster at the point we so often do in therapy of the
adolescent. It was at the point where he was obviously
struggling with conflicts over passivity as manifested in his
fear that somehow the therapist would change him too
much. Whereas one might argue that at this point therapy
could have begun in earnest, there is another side to the
issue. As his projection and externalization of conflict
was reduced, the patient had arrived at a point in therapy
where he openly and with much conscious awareness was
struggling with an adolescence-specific conflict over
passivity, a conflict over development of an independent

stance. This conflict was not one to be resolved in therapy but a conflict with which he needed to tussle and to work out over an extended period of time during the long span of adolescence within the multitude of his everyday interactions. In effect, psychotherapy is to help remove the roadblocks—if they are conflicts, to help resolve them—that interfere with the child's dealing or coping with his developmental task. The therapist errs if he tackles the age-specific developmental tasks and attendant conflicts without getting primarily at those forces which interfere with the youngster's natural coping mechanisms. In the process he may unwittingly take long, circuitous paths around problems which are probably amenable to therapeutic ventures but which are likely to become sealed over because not tended to.

Neubauer (Panel Report 1965) noted that "since one deals with an organization in continuous change, it is not always easy to know whether the disappearance of pathology is due to successful treatment or to psychic reorganization only to reoccur at a later time. How long therefore should one maintain contact with the child in order to achieve optimum resolution of conflicts?" Rangell (Panel Report 1965), on the same panel, noted that it is not right to prolong what Anthony (Panel Report 1965) calls "the open wound." He goes on to say that the analyst should resist the tendency to become the proud parent who may then unconsciously wish to hold the child throughout subsequent development and bask in the glory of the success of the analysis.

So as to emphasize further the need for a conceptual model for child psychotherapy, a few more comments about comparisons between adult and child psychotherapy are in order. To build a conceptual model on such comparisons is doomed to failure, as it leaves child psychotherapy fettered to a model that is inherently deficient. The end result is bound to be frustration and disillusionment. There is the disillusionment of the parents and of the child because they become victims of a process which does not suit their needs. Such conceptualization according to adult models also leads to disillusionment of the child

therapist who finds himself out of place and on the wrong frequency. This may very well be the reason why so many child
therapists "cop out" to adult psychotherapy where they can
more effectively treat patients according to the model of
psychotherapy they have developed for themselves. They
want to see the patient alone, without getting involved with
the family. They want to see him in an office where they
can concentrate on verbal content in a manner that is so
familiar to adults. They may find the adults' productions so
much easier to organize, and accordingly so much easier
to comprehend within their theoretical framework. The patient in turn seems to respond so much more obviously to
the usual interventions, i.e. he generally talks in a way that
makes sense to the therapist.

Joselyn has observed that "we frequently bemoan the fact
that child psychiatrists trained adequately in child psychiatry tend, as they go into private practice, to abandon
their children's work and focus more increasingly on adults."
She attributed this attention to be due in part to the fact
that "it is difficult to work with the many types of children
referred to the child psychiatrist unless there is more than
psychotherapy possible." However, might not this problem
also be the result of an inadequate conceptual model for
psychotherapy with children? If a therapist hangs onto the
adult model and is constantly falling back on comparisons,
why not drift back to adult work where the model fits more
adequately!

Lastly, difficulties in arriving at a conceptual model
for child psychotherapy may also reflect a vulnerability in
the practitioners themselves. Adults who work with children
may tend to have identity problems in their professional
work. There are a couple of routes by which the child
psychotherapist may go by virtue of his identity crisis. He
may strive to be or to become the benevolent parent who
is to compensate for those malevolent ones who have been
rearing his patients. Or he may unwittingly choose to
identify with the child. By this option he may, among other

things, become like a little man treating little people. In this role he may tend to become too self-effacing as he feels downtrodden and unappreciated by those "big doctors" who treat "big people." The child therapist then ends up spending his time trying to identify with those "big doctors" by doing what they do and thus following too closely the adult model of psychotherapy.

While this chapter has taken a broad panoramic view of child psychotherapy, the chapters to follow will deal with specific features of child psychotherapy. It is hoped that consideration of these features will help the child psychotherapist develop for himself a conceptual model within which to manage children and their families who come to him.

II

ASSESSMENT OF THE CHILD

THE PROTOTYPE of the diagnostic process in child therapy is found in the procedure adopted by child guidance clinics. In this setting the psychiatrist is considered leader of the team that includes, besides a psychiatrist, a social worker and a psychologist. In this arrangement the social worker sees the parents to garner the historical data and to assess the family situation. The psychologist administers the prescribed tests to determine intelligence quotient and/or to assess other areas of personality functioning. The psychiatrist examines the child. When all the professionals involved in the evaluation meet to integrate their findings, it is the psychiatrist who organizes the accumulated information and the insights derived by each of them to arrive at a diagnostic formulation and appropriate treatment plans.

Though this model continues to be used in child guidance clinics and other clinics for children, in much of private practice of child therapy the child therapist does the initial assessment of the child and his family by himself, and he calls on the assistance of other professionals only as he feels such assistance is indicated. For example, the child psychiatrist may in select instances ask for psychological testing so as to answer specific questions about the child's personality functioning. Generally it is expected of the child therapist in training that he himself develop skills in history taking and assessment of families through his own examination of parents. Such an arrangement comes about as a result of a number of factors. There are the practical considerations such as lack of ready availability of other professionals, time and financial considerations, plus problems of coordinating professional activities outside a clinic setting. But there is also the fact that the therapist learns that he many times can get a better "feel" for what is going on if he himself sees the various family members. He finds that the diagnostic process can many times become a more integrated one when one person is involved, as he proceeds from a more panoramic view that allows him to follow given cues to delve further into given areas or to avoid detours that may be interesting but much too far afield to be worthwhile.

There are three cardinal points for the therapist to keep in mind as he approaches a diagnostic assessment. First, he needs to appreciate that the patient presents with symptoms that make sense and are understood when viewed within terms of the patient's current personal and interpersonal adjustment plus within terms of his total past personal and interpersonal functioning. Therefore, the therapist attempts to find answers to the following question: How do this child's symptoms effect a dynamic equilibrium or homeostasis within himself and within his environment? From there he then strives to understand the origins of this maladaptive behavior in the child's past. Accordingly, the assessment includes investigation of the individual functioning of this child at the moment and the immediate environment on which he impinges and which impinges on him, plus investigation of the child's past in similar terms. Second, the therapist needs to appreciate that the diagnostic assessment is based on the establishment of an emotional bridge between the therapist and the patient. Accordingly, the effectiveness of the assessment will rest in large measure on the therapist's ability to establish this bridge. Third, if he is to proceed in any sort of rational manner, the therapist will need to organize his data within some general theory of personality functioning, be it oriented along psychoanalytic, behavioral, or organic theoretical lines. It is from this theoretical understanding that diagnostic formulations and treatment plans will follow.

Since the patient is a child, there also are several matters germane to childhood that the therapist needs to keep in mind in this diagnostic assessment. First is the fact that the child does not come of his own accord but is brought by a parent or someone else responsible for him. While the child may pose a problem to family, school authorities, and/or the community at large so that any one or all of them may have initiated the referral, the examiner may find that he is dealing with a reluctant patient who does not feel a need to be there. Second, it must be remembered that the child is still in a fluid state both physically and psychologically. Assessment therefore needs to be based on a true appreciation of development. To appreciate development is to pay attention not only to the child's current level of adjustment in comparison to what can be expected of a child at this particular stage. The therapist also needs to be mindful of the antecedents of the current level of the child's development and of what can be expected to unfold in subsequent development.

To speak of development is to entail the risk of becoming embroiled in the nature versus nurture controversy regarding a child's development. How much is the child's adjustment a product of environment and how much can it be traced back to constitutional factors? Hopefully the therapist remains mindful of the complex interactions involved at a multitude of levels so that he does not feel compelled to take sides in fruitless controversy bred of simplistic reductions. There are, however, a number of features that we do know about environmental influences and other specifics that we do know about constitutional factors. It becomes the therapist's task to attempt to integrate these known elements into his own conceptualization of a child's adjustment.

In reference to environmental factors, there are several basic assumptions with which the therapist approaches the diagnostic assessment of children. First, it must be recognized that the child's behavior, be it "good" or "bad," adaptive or maladaptive from a social standpoint, still does reflect his attempts to adapt. In this light, the child's personality initially reflects the results of an interaction between him and his environment; his behavior first of all represents in effect the arrival at a compromise between his particular wishes and the wishes and expectations of those responsible for his care. Gradually his behavior takes on the cast of an arrival of a compromise between his wishes and the prohibitions and expectations which he has developed within himself. Put another way, the early interpersonal homeostatic attempts shape the intrapersonal, intrapsychic, homeostatic adjustment that follows. Implicit in this assumption is the idea that to ever greater degrees as the child's personality develops, any given behavior needs to be viewed as more than the mere product of his environment. I will say more about this later.

A second basic assumption is that the family can be viewed as a homeostatic unit in which the individual members arrive at a balance together in the multitude of their interactions. If each member is also to strike a balance within himself in such an arrangement so as to arrive at a reasonable emotional adjustment, it is important that each member be able to find in effect a suitable niche within the family with an opportunity generally to develop adequate emotional expression. While there is a need for an intimacy among the various family members, there is also a need for them to see each other as distinct individuals, each with his own particular needs, wishes, and potential. With the above in mind, it can be seen that a breakdown in this homeostatic family structure because of inordinate stress of one variety or another can be expected to be reflected in a breakdown in the emotional adjustment of one of its members who in effect may become the family's "sacrificial lamb." (This is not to deny that the converse may also be the case, namely, that a breakdown in the emotional adjustment of one of the members may be reflected in a disruption in the homeostatic balance of the family.) If one member does carry the burden in this regard, chances are that he is likely to be one of the children.

Third, if there is a true appreciation of the interaction between the parents and the children in the above sense, the therapist will look for how each contributes to the end result when problems do arise in the family. He recognizes that it is unrealistic to separate the family into the "good guys" and the "bad guys," the victims and the oppressors. He does not side with the parents nor does he side with the child. To take sides with the child and to see him as the innocent victim is the most common error among those who deal with problems of children so that this tendency even becomes an occupational hazard among those who work with children.

The fact is that the therapist is least likely to err if he approaches the family's problems with the assumption that somehow both the parent and the child are involved in whatever might be the unfortunate situation, be they wittingly or unwittingly so involved. The need to proceed in such a manner will be especially important when the therapist is confronted with a family in which it appears as though the child is picked on or scapegoated. He is likely to discover in such a situation that the "victimized" child is a polished provocateur who has himself cozily locked in a sado-masochistic relationship that he needs to maintain.

If the therapist views the family in the above prescribed manner, he can more freely become the more objective, nonpartisan helper who is not tied down by a need to pass judgment on family members. He is then in a position to study the manner in which they interact and with his "nonprosecutory" confrontations be in a better position to help the individual family members assess the type and the degree of investment each of them contributes to the clinical picture.

Such an approach to the family is more realistic in yet another sense. The therapist soon discovers that he most ordinarily deals with parents who are consciously dedicated but who have problems with their children because of unconscious factors that curtail or impede their ability to meet the demands of parenthood. In effect, they are saddled with immaturities in their own personality functioning. Again it will be the therapist's task to look beyond the manifest behavior and to look for determinants other than conscious volition. For example, the therapist may have the option to become angry with the manifestly rejecting mother or to empathize with her as the frustrated mother who never has been able to mother this particular child.

In reference to parental immaturities, there are four general areas to investigate so as to understand how the parents may be involved in their children's problems. First, there are the number of identifications and cross-identifications between the parent and the child; second, the parent's unresolved conflicts that hamper his overall functioning as a mature individual; third, the parent's unresolved conflicts that hamper his ability to function as an effective parent in a given situation or at a particular stage in the child's development; and fourth, emotional disturbance in the parent at a particular stage in the child's development though not specifically related to his interaction with his child. All these factors will be discussed in detail in the chapter "Family Considerations."

From nurture to nature—what are the constitutional factors to consider? In this regard, at the risk of sounding pedantic, it might be said that the therapist at least needs to remain mindful that the child is born with a basic physiological makeup in which psychological functioning will find its foundation and upon which it will unfold. The aim is to emphasize at this point that a given newborn infant is more than an amorphous piece of clay that passively awaits the artisan hand of the parent to shape his form.

More specifically, there are studies of neonates to keep in mind. In his observation of newborns, Wolff observes how the neonate appears to have his own particular rate and mode of nervous system discharge that is manifested in spontaneous motor patterns which include startles, sobbing inspirations, gentle lip movements, erections, transient smiles, and twitches of the face and small muscle groups of the limbs. How do these "preferred" channels of discharge during early infancy correlate with later differences in behavior? He notes that "a preponderance of either rhythmical mouthing or erections in infancy might predispose the older person to discharge tension (in a totally different sense) by similar channels motivated to act in response to inner need." It remains to be understood to what extent early spontaneous behaviors might be integrated into and how they might influence later purposeful behaviors. Fries has demonstrated how newborns react differently in terms of the degree of startle response to a standard stimulus. Degree of reaction lay on a continuum from hypoactive to hyperactive response, but each infant showed a relative constancy in the extent of his response to repeated tests. Lipton and his workers have illustrated how the quality and the quantity of autonomic system response to a standard stimulus varies from one neonate to another, but the type and the degree of response is specific to the individual child. For example, when he studied infants' changes in heart rate in response to a waft of air directed to the abdomen, he found individual specific differences among children in terms of the time it took a child to respond, the extent of heart rate change, and the time it took the child to return to a pretest rate.

How does one resolve the nature-nurture controversy regarding child development? Perhaps the individual therapist is likely to follow the route taken by the evolution of theories on child development, which is, as Ausubel notes, that more current formulations of the respective roles of heredity and environment in development are couched in more interactional terms. As such, the emphasis shifts from the "all-or-none" propositions to estimates of the overall relative importance. He then offers guidelines by which one might arrive at an understanding of the interactional process.

> The respective roles of hereditary and environmental factors in the bipolar regulation of development may be summarized in the following listing of the ways in which each participates in the developmental process:

> 1. Genic factors set absolute *limits* of growth for both in-

dividual and species which cannot be exceeded in any environment, as well as determine capacity for profiting from environmental stimulation. Environmental factors similarly *limit* the extent to which genic potentiality can be realized in individuals or species. In a generally optimal environment, phenotypic (description of the organism in terms of its observable qualities) actualization of the genotype (genic endowment or the totality of inherited elements) is enhanced for everyone, and the prevailing range of variability is widened.

2. Both factors in varying degrees contribute to the *patterning* of traits, i. e. determining the direction, differentiation, content and sequence of development.

3. Gene variables make the individual *selectively* sensitive to or more prone to prefer certain aspects of the environment to others. Environmental variables, on the other hand, in accordance with cultural needs and values, differentially *select* from the total range of genic potentiality certain capacities and traits for maximal development and others for relative oblivion.

4. To a certain extent, the genically conditioned temperamental characteristics of an individual help determine his environment by differentially affecting the attitudes and reactions toward himself of significant persons in his interpersonal milieu.

Without apology for his stand, the therapist in his psychotherapeutic endeavors is essentially an environmentalist. How he is so, however, perhaps needs clearer definition. He proceeds as an environmentalist in the sense that he attempts to undo and/or redo experiences that have helped to shape the child. The aim is to help this child patient reorganize his particular personality functioning so that his behavior is more adaptive. The ultimate aim of this therapy, as posited earlier in this book, is to establish the development of awareness as a powerful assist to mastery of self.

While a determination of the relative potency of environmental and constitutional, hereditary factors ultimately is important for the development of means to assist people more realistically and more effectively, concentration on constitutional factors ordinarily is not within the domain of the psychotherapist in his work. However, he ought to be imbued with an appreciation of constitutional factors as he proceeds in his task of therapy. Accordingly, he ought to start out with the appreciation that in the face of emotional turmoil, as in the face of other stress in life, people are inclined to do what comes naturally and that which comes naturally is ordinarily founded in constitutional predispositions. The expression of these predispositions then becomes heightened or diminished through childhood experiences. Furthermore, expression of predisposition, be it toward hyperactivity or toward reticence, for example, may be heightened when used as a defense against affect like anxiety or depression. The aim in psychotherapy ordinarily is not to tackle the predisposition but to elicit an exaggeration or a diminution of some particular behavioral expression.

Accordingly, the therapist ordinarily need not get caught up in an argument of constitution and heredity versus environment. The more he is involved in such controversy the more he is likely to err in one of two directions. If he takes the side of environment, he is likely to be a therapist who feels that in therapy children can be changed in the sense that traits can be eliminated and others implanted rather than children changed in the sense that there is a realignment of personality functioning with emphasis toward mastery through conscious awareness. If he takes a firm stand on constitution, he may be a moralist in disguise who assumes a benevolent role as he essentially tries to dismiss personal responsibility for particular behavior by labelling it constitutional.

DIAGNOSTIC PROCESS

The patient is introduced to the therapist initially through the symptoms for which he has been referred. These symptoms ordinarily include the multitude of behavioral problems that most commonly consist of variations on the theme of hyperactivity, coupled with inadequate conformity, learning problems, the various neurotic symptoms (phobias, obsessions, and compulsions), and various somatic symptoms that defy medical explanation or are felt to be part of a psychophysiological disorder. Most ordinarily it is behavior that precipitates referral, and most commonly it is a variety of behavior that either gets the child in trouble with others or at least attracts someone's attention to him. To the unsophisticated, either he may be a "pain" of one sort or another or his behavior is "bizarre"; to the more sophisticated, his behavior may be seen to reflect unhappiness and tension.

Ordinarily the therapist can rely on an interview with the parents to obtain his history about the child's symptoms and overall adjustment. In addition it may also be helpful to obtain pertinent history about the child from school and other community sources if the child's problems have spilled over to outside his home. To contact these latter sources for information may even be essential when the focus of the child's problems has been in school and/or in the community at large. In this regard it is not unusual to find that a child does not come to anyone's attention as a disturbed child until he is enrolled in school. When the teacher is then concerned about the child, the family may be nonplussed about the school's request for psychiatric consultation. An illustration of such a family is seen in the following clinical vignette.

> Judy was a five-year-old girl on whom the school requested psychiatric referral because of her bizarre behavior at school. Judy talked in an expressionless manner, and for the most part she looked very much preoccupied. Motorically she appeared disjointed as she moved about awkwardly. She was a relative loner among the children, as she did not seem to know how to play with them. During structured activities in kindergarten she was attentive for only brief periods of time, as most of the time she talked aloud and moved around the classroom as though driven by her whims of the moment.
>
> In contrast to the school's marked concern, which was legitimate enough, as Judy proved to be a severely disturbed girl with many autistic features in her behavior, the parents initially were impassive about her. They were not concerned about her development, erratic as it had been, and they found her to be "no problem" at home.

Such examples again point to the need to see a child within the context of his family and to see what role he plays in this family. It turned out that Judy fit well in her family in which all the members were inclined to be at least a bit "different" even while they interacted well together and showed adequate social adjustment. In another instance it may be found that objectively gross disturbance can go unheeded in the family because it is needed and therefore fostered by a family that maintains its psychological homeostasis through significant maladjustment of one of its members. This is not to say, however, that every discrepancy in the report of the family compared to that from the extrafamilial source points to denial of one variety or another in the family. It is understandable, for example, that a child may manifest difficulties in school and in that manner present a picture there which is objectively different from the one he projects at home. He may feel freer to "let loose" in school for one reason or another, or he may even feel compelled to do so. It may also be that the child has "something going" with a teacher or teachers in general for one reason or other. It may be that the child displaces his conflicts with his parents onto his relationships with teachers or with a particular teacher. However, there are also instances in which a teacher may "misidentify" a child and in doing so may help elicit problematic behavior in that manner because of her own unresolved conflicts.

A gross example of a teacher's distorted reaction to a child is seen in the case of a latency-age boy who was referred for psychiatric evaluation after he allegedly drew an obscene picture in art class. He had been a thorn in the teacher's side because of repeated disruptive behavior, but she felt a need to refer him for psychiatric evaluation only after he allegedly drew a picture of a boy with his penis exposed. This picture was never discussed with the boy nor was it shown to his parents. Rather the school social worker presented it in person to the psychiatrist in the clinic at the time of the evaluation. To the surprise of the psychiatrist and to the embarrassment of the social worker, the boy in the picture was obviously wearing a gun in holster, strategically placed near his genital area. As it turned out, the problem child was not nearly as "loose and unglued" as the school feared him to be.

Once again the task is not to look for discrepancies so as to ferret out the culprit in the saga of the problem child. Rather the aim should be to understand the interactional patterns so as to gain insight into the origins and perpetuation of the problems that have precipitated referral. The fact is that the therapist may obtain a realistic picture of what has transpired only after he gets some idea of how the interaction among the various people concerned—child, parents, teacher—is colored by the particular distortions that each introduces into this interaction.

While it would appear that the therapist hardly needs to be reminded of the necessity to obtain a detailed chronology of the problems for which a child is referred for evaluation, the importance of not proceeding on the basis of assumptions regarding obtainable history is highlighted in clinical examples like the following one. Sue ended up in outpatient psychotherapy after she allegedly started several fires, including one that extensively destroyed a neighbor's home. In the fourth month of therapy, as the therapist became ever more disbelieving that Sue would have committed arson as had been claimed, he finally learned that Sue had confessed to the crime after two and a half hours of interrogation by a fire inspector. Originally the parents had sought psychiatric treatment with an urgency that had led the therapist to believe that there was not the slightest shadow of a doubt that Sue had set the fire, as circumstantial evidence was capped by a confession, details of which the therapist had erroneously not explored.

In other instances it may be found that the parents will be quick to discuss many areas of concern for which they previously had never felt a need to seek help rather than dwell on the problems for which they now are moved to seek consultation. Many times it may be very appropriate to determine how much the parents' ready discussion of other problem areas reflects the fact that their child's recent behavior was "the straw that broke the camel's back" and how much it reflects avoidance of the problem at hand by concentration on other matters—a pattern that the parents may have regularly followed with the result that problems have become compounded rather than resolved. Or the parents may attempt to have their child engaged in psychotherapy as a means to expiate their own feelings of guilt even as they have the therapist assume a role that they more realistically ought to assume. It is as though now that their child is in therapy they can brush their hands clean and proceed peacefully.

There is the danger that as a therapist stresses the need to work on more general problems in a child's personality functioning so as to help him resolve some particular problems for which he presents, and as he deemphasizes the possibility that there are problems which lend themselves to more immediate and more direct resolution, he unwittingly may not focus sharply enough on the presenting problems. It is easy enough to forget that the route to personality reorganization, if that is the goal, is through dealing with specific items, specific problems, as investigation and resolution of these specific problems touches on broader areas of personality functioning. Changes in dealing with these specific problems ought then to impinge on the child's overall personality structure with a gradual realignment toward more adaptive functioning.

The task then in an assessment of a child is to start with a detailed account of the present so as to have a clear picture of what is happening currently in this child and in his total environment. While it appears that those who counsel children and families often err by concentrating too much on the present without understanding past determinants, closer examination is likely to show that concentrating on the present is not of itself the mistake. Rather the error is likely to lie in proceeding from abstractions, generalizations, and assumptions so that the therapist does not have a detailed picture of the scene into which he intrudes himself. This is not to underestimate the necessity for a longitudinal view if the therapist is to have some idea of the adaptive patterns that have emerged and the problem areas that impede the child and his family. Only with some understanding in this regard can the therapist proceed with some rhyme, reason, and assurance as to where and how he ought to proceed, i.e. direct dealing with the problem, direct problem resolution with assistance in particular areas of personality functioning, or attempts at more general personality reorganization.

As intimated above, the complete report of the child's difficulties from all concerned plus the examination of the child will give a cross-sectional view of him at this time in his life span. However, a longitudinal view is also in order if the present is to be seen in perspective, and it is this view which is obtained in the developmental history. Without the longitudinal, developmental view and with emphasis on the cross-sectional current adjustment or maladjustment, the therapist is likely to either overestimate or underestimate the severity of the problem at hand or may even be hard pressed to delineate the nature of the problem.

The therapist might pursue developmental history with the idea that the "big picture" of the child includes the following facets. First, what is and what has been the parents' image of this child and in turn how does and how may have their image of him influenced his development both positively and negatively? (More will be said about this facet in Chapter V.) Second, what has been this child's view of himself and the world, and in turn how has he structured his world since the dawn of his psychological functioning? Third, from a relatively objective standpoint, what sort of child is this and what has been his particular life style? What constitutes his particular coping mechanisms? In turn, how have his life style and coping mechanisms made him vulnerable, and how have they become reflected in symptom formation? In this context, symptom formation would be viewed as maladaptive behavior either in terms of the child's diminished personal efficiency and/or in terms of his maladjustment within his family or within society at large.

Rather than view the child himself in terms of his particular coping style, there is danger that the therapist may be inclined to look at coping styles judgmentally with the notion that one way of coping is legitimate while another is not or that one style is more desirable than another. The task is to appreciate that there are a variety of coping styles and that each style has its own particular assets while it carries its own particular vulnerabilities. There are children who approach a problem cautiously as they in effect weigh the situation carefully before they proceed, while there are others who plunge headlong to tackle a problem aggressively. This point of the above is illustrated in the following clinical vignette.

Mrs. M. sought psychiatric consultation regarding her two sons on the recommendation of their nursery school teachers who were concerned about the level of the boys' adjustment even while neither was felt to exhibit major problems at the moment. Five-year-old Tom was fairly aggressive in school. He was quick to get in battles with other children, and he was inclined to do what pleased his fancy at the moment rather than go along with the requests of his teacher. In contrast, his four-year-old brother Mark was observed to be quiet and inclined to withdraw by himself. The teacher saw Mark to be shy, and she repeatedly felt a need to "draw him out."

In her written comments, Mark's teacher clearly spelled out how he seemed unsure of himself, how he appeared in need of reassurance and of how he did engage in activities many times only after she invited him to do so. Among the comments descriptive of Tom's aggressive behavior, his teacher noted how he responded well in activities that won him praise. She recommended to his parents that they engage him in activities that would earn him praise at home.

The common thread through the two reports was the element of insecurity, openly mentioned in the description of Mark but alluded to in comments about Tom. Why the two boys evidenced some heightened feelings of insecurity is not germane to our discussion at the moment. Rather the point to dwell on is the differing life styles of the two boys. The picture that emerged in further discussion with the mother was the fact that Mark was generally inclined to be cautious and to retreat a bit in the face of a stress or of a problem while Tom was found to attack new situations or problem areas rather impulsively.

Briefly, a major part of the consultation centered around reviewing with the mother how her two sons responded with different styles to the stresses of nursery school and home, how each child could cope effectively in his own particular way but also how each tended to get into difficulty in a different manner through his particular style. Specifically, counselling regarding management centered around the mother's need to tune in on the feelings of insecurity each of her children manifested. With Mark she would need to encourage him and assist him to move forward to meet a problem rather than to become frozen in an entrenched position. With Tom she would also need to help him appreciate his sense of insecurity, but in contrast to her management of Mark, she would need to discourage his tendency to defend against such awareness by reliance on activity and to help him learn to temper his aggressive attack of a problem with a bit of deliberation.

With these facets in mind the therapist is ready to proceed with the specifics of obtaining a developmental history. The most commonly pursued specifics are data like ages at which the child attained various milestones such as sitting alone, standing, walking, talking, and completion of toilet training. They also include presence or absence of phenomena like thumb sucking, rocking, temper tantrums, and various fears. While such data are somewhat descriptive of a child, to concentrate on it by itself may become an inadequate substitute for actually thinking in truly developmental terms. To think in developmental terms is to think in terms of dynamic interplay in regards to intrapersonal and interpersonal functioning. It is to appreciate that the attainment of a milestone and the presence or absence of a phenomenon (symptom, if you will) is not the prime consideration. Rather the manner of attainment of a milestone and the manner in which behavior ordinarily considered symptomatic fits into the child's overall adjustment become important to the therapist who wishes to understand the process of the child's development rather than to merely catalogue the end products of the developmental process. In effect, the therapist tries to obtain a fuller understanding of a child's current level of adjustment by getting to understand what adaptive patterns have emerged and how they developed. From here he hopes to deduce more realistically the relative strength of various personality functions. Secondarily, the understanding of the child's development ought to help him make more reasonable recommendations, with or without the assistance of some form of psychotherapy.

The search for dynamic factors might best be organized around attempts to understand how and to what extent the child has mastered the various developmental tasks with which he has been confronted. Such an approach proceeds in a manner similar to A. Freud's (1965) assessment of a child in terms of developmental lines. According to her model, a child is assessed in terms of his mastery of various personality tasks, e.g. growth and development from a dependent stance to a relatively independent position, rather than through attempts to study particular ego and superego functions in isolation. Accordingly, the following is offered as a framework within which to organize the history-taking process and the material derived thereof.

The first task in the neonatal period and well into the first year of life might be considered to be the establishment of the foundations to be able to enjoy instinctual gratifications. The building blocks would seem to include satisfying feeding experiences, the experience of resting peacefully and the experience of being comforted when in distress. To be comforted would seem to include not only the mother's care in this regard but also the utilization of autoerotic activities such as thumb sucking. With this in mind, the therapist might think in terms of answering the following questions regarding the child's earliest adjustment. What were the child's experiences at birth and in the neonatal period? As a neonate, what sort of basic constitutional predisposition did he seem to manifest? Did he tend to be hypoactive or hyperactive? Did he tend toward irritability or complacency? How did he react to frustration? How did he respond to ministrations in his frustration? Did he respond to maternal efforts to comfort him? Did he have autoerotic "pacifiers" at his disposal? If so, did he need to rely on them in place of maternal care or were they available for supplementary use? How much were his parents able to tolerate the child's engagement in auto-erotic activities? When and how was weaning from the breast and/or bottle accomplished?

The second task in the first year of life and one that poses itself more or less coincidentally with the above mentioned is the establishment of the foundations for object relation-ships. The following are the sorts of questions that might help assess the mastery of this task: Did he respond to at-tention from mother, father and others responsible for his care? Did he offer feedback that made him appealing and invited an object relationship? Did he proceed to the devel-opment of a symbiotic tie with his mother? Indications for this development are the appearance of separation anxiety and the fear of strangers at approximately eight months of age and its persistence into the latter part of the second year. Absence of these phenomena needs to be investigated further.

The next task up the development line includes individua-tion and mastery of aggression. There is merit in considering the two processes together, as in many ways the two go hand in hand. Even as the child begins to tolerate his mother's ab-sence such as her leaving him with a baby-sitter for the eve-ning, he begins to respond to demands made of him with a universal "No!" It is through negation that he originally af-firms and confirms his separateness. The therapist might look for answers to the following questions regarding this stage of development. How have the parents been inclined to deal with the child's early aggressive "explorations" of his envi-rons and how have they been inclined to deal with his neg-ativistic expressions? Questions about the timing of and the manner of toilet training are important but ought to be part of a more general inquiry about how the parents managed the child's early aggressive experiences. As he has developed locomotion and has met up with obstacles to his aggression, what have been his responses to frustration? In his early "trial runs" with his aggression, it can be expected that a child may persistently pursue the "forbidden fruit" and that he may throw temper tantrums in response to frustration. Have his parents been able to deal with such behavior in a spirit of tolerance with allowances made for his immaturities? Have they made attempts to help him deal with his frustrations so as to develop reasonable means to handle them, or have his parents been inclined to deal with his frustrations by giving in to his original demands unreasonable as they might have been? May the emphasis have been placed on curtailing aggressive activity so as to avoid frustration? Might he have been left to his own meager resources to deal with his feelings of frustration? Or may the parents have tended to turn their backs on their child's behavior so that he has been left on his own to learn how to be reasonably aggressive? Has he had the opportunity to learn to say "No" to certain behavioral expressions even while there is opportunity for him to learn to channel his interests in suitable directions? Have the parents helped him begin to learn to discriminate between a wish and the gratification of this wish, between feelings and expression of these feelings?

Whereas earlier the child can be expected to be aggressive many times virtually in an attempt to display aggression or try out his power, as he has proceeded into the nursery school have there been more evidences of goal-directed manifestations of aggression? Correspondingly has there been a diminution in the display of diffuse aggression seen in temper tantrums and in play in which there is wholesale destruction? Has this manifestation of goal-directed aggression been associated with emergence of spontaneous, relatively uninhibited curiosity? What has been the parents' stance regarding these developments?

If the therapist looks on the task of the preschool age (ages 3 to 5) in terms of the initial consolidation of sexual gender, several questions need to be answered. Has the child had the opportunity to become comfortably aware of genital sexuality in terms of anatomy and in terms of opportunity to acquaint himself with his anatomy? Have there been indications of a natural inclination toward sexual identification with the parent of the same sex or has he been inclined to identify in the opposite direction? If the latter is true, has it resulted from absence of a parent or difficulties and disruptions in a comfortable relationship with one or the other of the parents? Has the child evolved a comfortable relationship in his family so that he in effect remains in the position of a child though in comfortable "competition" with his parents? Or have the parents in one way or another relinquished to the child their role of parent? In his emergence as more truly a social being, has he evidenced an ability to play with siblings and peers in activities that involve a mutual interaction?

As the child has entered school have there been evidences that the child has adequately mastered impulse awareness and age-appropriate impulse expression so that he has enjoyed an internal relative quietude that has allowed for learning? Or has he given indications of an inhibition of these impulses or of a raw expression of them, due to unresolved conflicts in either event, that in turn has led to learning difficulties or varying degrees of fruitless engagement in the learning process? In this school-age period the therapist needs to focus not only on the child's cognitive development but also on his social development, which takes on new dimensions as the child moves into an expanded world of multiplied interactions with peers and teachers. The initial big test of the ability to socialize does come with the child's entrance to school, as his ability to interact reasonably with teachers and peers gives an indication of the nature of his developing object relationships. Accordingly, the therapist needs to explore the following areas. Have there been school-refusal problems that to varying degrees point to relatively incomplete dissolution of his earlier symbiotic tie with his mother? Has persistently obstructive sibling rivalry or infantile self-centeredness been reflected in an inability to be *a* member of the class rather than *the* member of the class who demands a teacher's undivided attention? Have there been evidences of unresponsiveness to the teacher, excessive dependence on her, and/or various types of provocative behavior with teachers and peers that further point to problems in development of object relationships?

The nature of the child's development in socialization and in his object relationships is further assessed with the aid of data about his friendships and other social contacts outside the home. Has he had friends? What type of friends has he attracted and what type of friendships has he sought? Have his friends been exclusively children of his sex or have they included children of the opposite sex? Since the child of grade-school age ordinarily restricts his friendships with children of his same sex, may precocious heterosexual pursuits have served as a defense against homosexual yearnings? Has he played with friends his own age or does he gravitate to younger or older children? The therapist might keep in mind that the child's preference for play with younger children may point to pseudo-adult behavior as well as a wish for return to earlier days. Similarly, play with older children may reflect passive yearnings or a leap to a more advanced stage in order to avoid current conflicts at this stage of development.

As puberty approaches, what have appeared to be the child's responses to the early stirrings of genital feelings and urges? If a girl, what have her reactions been to menarche? If a boy, how has he reacted to his "wet dreams"? How has the child responded to masturbatory urges? What might have been the nature of his particular conflicts over masturbation? The therapist ought to keep in mind that it is common to find children to have a variety of neurotic symptoms and manifestations of regressed behavior around the time of puberty in response to early sexual strivings.

As the child proceeds further into adolescence, there is more to be learned about his sexual experiences and what they have meant to him. Fantasies, for example, associated with masturbation are helpful if one is to understand the nature of the adolescent's intrapsychic organization of genital sexuality, but the therapist needs to be aware that such fantasies ordinarily are not gleaned in early contacts with the relatively intact adolescent. Or the therapist may find that the adolescent boy, for example, relates the "right" fantasies, as he has learned that a boy is "supposed" to think about girls when he masturbates.

How has the adolescent mastered his aggressive tendenies which initially for him are in the service of individuation much as was the case early in life? In what manner have yearnings for independence manifested themselves and how has he proceeded toward the attainment of a relatively independent stance? In this regard, what have been the manifestations of his identity crisis which follows on the heels of the "second individuation" process? Has the relative dissolution of inner infantile attachments culminated in an ability to strive for his own particular identity? Or much like the two-year-old, has he settled for an identity based on negativism or on a display of aggression for aggression's sake without an ability to channel it into goal-directed activity?

A number of factors ought to be kept in mind to explore when appropriate as the therapist proceeds in his investigation of development. There is the family and/or other settings in which the child was reared that needs to be understood. In the broadest sense, in what ways has the family facilitated the developmental process and in what ways may it have impeded or distorted this process? More specifically, how intact has the family been during this child's life? What is the nature of the problems with which they have had to cope? To get into this area of specifics is to get onto a subject discussed in detail in Chapter V. The point to be made here is that the therapist is not to aim to merely catalogue the stresses with which the family has been confronted, rather he ought to try to understand what may have been their impact on the child's development. This understanding is based on an appreciation that to understand the impact of the stress is to understand the nature of the stress in con-

junction with the child's and his parents' particular manner
of coping with the particular stress and their specific vulnerabilities at that moment. For example, while the loss of his
mother during the height of his symbiotic tie with her can
be expected to have its impact on the child, the eventual developmental outcome will be determined by a host of factors
other than the loss itself.

Another factor to keep in mind is the fate of various
symptom formations during the course of development. The
therapist ought to try to understand the nature of these symptoms along with the reasons for their occurrence and their
eventual course, in the sense that they are maladaptive means
of dealing with particular conflicts. Ordinarily it is to be expected that a child may manifest temporary symptom formations that represent a transient maladaptive turn in time of
stress, be it a developmental crisis variety or otherwise, but
it is also to be expected that these symptoms may be given
up as a more comfortable position is attained. Such, for example, is the case with symptoms like phobias in the pre-
school-age child and with various obsessive-compulsive symptoms in the school-age child. In a sense, the task is to differentiate between transient neurotic reactions and relatively
consolidated neuroses in which there are fixations at earlier
stages of development and rigid patterns of adjustment that
impede further development.

It also needs to be remembered that childhood symptoms
may be misleading because they ordinarily do not proceed
unaltered into adulthood. Either the nature of the manifest
symptom changes or one extreme leads to another in a misleading manner; the underlying turmoil persists as the child's
conflicts remain unaltered, even while his observable behavior changes. For example, the phobia of childhood may be
transformed into obsessive-compulsive neurotic behavior in
adulthood. Impulsive early school-age behavior gives way to
school-age compulsivity though reasonable expression of aggression remains unattainable. Accordingly, it needs to be
determined whether symptom disappearance reflects resolu-

tion of conflict or whether it reflects substitution by other maladaptation such as new symptom formation, developmental stunting, or inhibition so as to avoid painful stress but which may further establish the child's emotional vulnerability.

Another factor to consider in conjunction with a child's development is his physiological state over the years. What illnesses and injuries have befallen him? Again the therapist might pose for himself a variety of questions that include the following: How has the child dealt with these? Did he evidence anxiety under such stress? What were his obvious and/or disguised manifestations of anxiety? Did their disappearance reflect mastery or retreat to a comfortable but emotionally vulnerable position? At what stage of development were these bodily insults experienced and what may have been their impact on his future development? Have they retarded or accelerated development? What has stunting at this stage done to future developmental phases?

PHYSICAL EXAMINATION

Most typically in child therapy units the physical examination of the child is done by someone other than the examining psychiatrist. The importance and even the necessity for this part of the assessment of the child will vary from situation to situation and even realistically may depend upon the therapist's orientation. It is easy enough to say that the therapist needs at least to be aware of the physical status of the child and that adequate assessment is out of the question without an awareness of the physiological state of the child. However, such a statement may be meaningless, and the therapist may make it primarily in an attempt to curry favor or to convince others that he is thorough, even while he appreciates that so many childhood psychiatric problems occur without discernible or physically modifiable physiological changes. Furthermore, this fact is many times ascertainable from the historical material alone even if the child presents primarily with physical symptoms.

The therapist does need to be realistically thorough in his assessment of the child's physiological state, and such thoroughness ordinarily involves considerably less than diagnostic study just short of a brain biopsy. The aim ought to be for the therapist to arrive at a position where he can feel reasonably comfortable about the relative importance of physiological forces operative in this child before he proceeds to concentrate primarily on psychological forces, the latter being the legitimate task of psychotherapy. If he does not start from such a relatively secure position, he may find that therapy will begin to flounder, either because of his own disturbing doubts or those of his patient or of the patient's parents. The point is that all concerned, the therapist as well as the child and his parents, need to feel confident about the diagnosis.

In regards to the therapist, he will need to deal comfortably with physical symptoms that emerge or reappear or that are aggravated during the course of therapy. To refer a patient for further diagnostic evaluation during the course of therapy is one thing if such referral is prompted by the onset of new symptoms that defy explanation; it is still another matter to pause midway in therapy to further evaluate symptoms that were incompletely assessed before therapy began. As for the patient, he and his family may initially need to believe that his emotional problems are caused by some physical aberration. Subsequently because of what they perceive to be inadequate physical examination, they may be left with doubts that smolder beneath the surface only to flare up as a powerful resistance later in the course of therapy. If the family is inclined to concentrate on physical causes at the expense of psychological factors so as to avoid what they consider to be an admission of failure, the therapist might find it especially difficult to pursue assessment in a reasonable fashion. While he, for example, seeks appropriate consultations and laboratory studies, the family may attempt to force his hand to prolong diagnostic assessment in hopes that some physical cause will be found to which the problem can be attributed. In such a a case, only after especial deliberation the therapist ought to proceed with further studies lest in his tendency to attempt to placate the family with more tests that are of no value, or of questionable value at best, he end up appearing as though he, too, is not convinced of the influence of psychological factors. An illustration of this point is seen in the following clinical example.

Roberta was a thirteen-year-old girl who was referred for psychiatric care because of her intermittent blindness, i.e. a constriction of her visual fields so that it was like "looking down two tubes" ushered in brief periods of total blindness.

By the time the psychiatrist saw her, she had been examined by the family pediatrician and an ophthalmologist, and both were in agreement that there was no physical abnormality to account for her symptoms.

There was the fact that her symptoms just did not follow physiological patterns as well as indications that these symptoms occurred under the stress of sexual excitement which further led the resident psychiatrist and his supervisor to conclude that the referring physician's diagnosis of conversion reaction was realistic enough. However, the parents proved to be unaccepting of this diagnosis at this point and requested further tests. It was on their request that the resident did take upon himself to order an EEG, as he thought nothing was to be lost if it took but one more negative test to reassure the parents. However, the parents responded to the negative EEG report as the resident's supervisor had originally anticipated; namely, they still were not satisfied with the diagnosis and requested further examinations that would include skull films and biochemical assays. Rather than order more tests, the resident psychiatrist now discussed with the parents their need to look for organic causes to account for their daughter's symptoms. The end result was that they then did accept the diagnosis and did agree to a course of what proved to be successful psychotherapy.

Ordinarily there is no great problem deciding upon a reasonably adequate physical assessment. Problems do arise, however, if the therapist is afflicted with a need to diagnose a disorder as either a physical or a psychological problem. There certainly are many childhood disorders that cry for absolutistic explanation, be it embedded in physical or psychological theory, as they entail phenomena that so often defy satisfactory explanation. Such is the case with various behavior disorders, learning problems, and psychotic disorders of childhood. It is with these sorts of problems that the one who focuses well-nigh exclusively on physical causes may be unreasonably complete in his physiological assessments even as he ignores glaring psychological factors, while the purveyor of psychological explanations may unreasonably abbreviate physiological assessments that might conceivably lead to more reasonable rehabilitative planning. Unfortunately, disputatious rancor from these devotees to absolute positions may be a poor substitute for the meeting of the minds to try to integrate the understanding and management of complicated, frustrating problems.

There is an error that may be shared by those who assess children, regardless of the orientation toward children's problems, an error that may lead to unreasonable approaches to physical assessment. That is the error of making a diagnosis of bona fide emotional disorder primarily by exclusion of physical causes to account for the problem at hand. Such an approach not only leads to erroneous diagnoses but it also serves to downgrade the significance of emotional factors, as the diagnosis of emotional disorders is reserved for conditions in which there is no readily ascertainable physical abnormality. This approach does not lend itself to realistic consideration of the coexistence of physical and psychological abnormalities. An error that may result from such an approach to diagnostic assessment is illustrated in the following clinical example.

Susan was a thirteen-year-old girl who was referred for psychiatric evaluation with a diagnosis of a "psychosomatic disorder" after her physicians could find no physical cause for her persistently painful stiff right knee. While no organic pathology could be demonstrated on physical examination, x-ray, and other laboratory studies, Susan walked and sat with her leg hyperextended at the knee. On physical examination Susan did complain of excruciating pain when her leg was flexed at the knee, but her grossly melodramatic response had her examiners wonder how much of and even whether the pain was for real. Her pediatrician even commented, "When you attempt to examine her she cries as though she were about to lose something."

There was no doubt that Susan had a definite hysterical bent about her so that she looked as though she should have a conversion reaction if she did not have one. There also were some possible psychological explanations for her knee problem on a symbolic level, such as onset of the pain without obvious trauma while on an outing with her divorced mother and the mother's husband-to-be, plus a possible identification with a younger brother who suffered from cerebral palsy that especially afflicted one of his legs. However, the consulting psychiatrist did not feel convinced of the diagnosis of conversion reaction, because there appeared to be some signs of pathology in her knee even while the exact nature could not be determined at the moment, and specific psychological evidence was not sufficient to substantiate a diagnosis of conversion reaction. Nonetheless, he did begin to see her in therapy explicitly to get at problems that might be reflected in her knee problem.

After six months of therapy Susan was cured of her "conversion reaction" when the attending orthopedic surgeon corrected a dislocating patella condition that had finally been discovered in a follow-up physical examination. Unfortunately, he also convinced the mother to discontinue Susan's psychotherapy, as he flatly told her that Susan no longer needed to see a psychiatrist since he now had discovered the cause of Susan's knee trouble. Actually, initially it would have been more realistic for the therapist to address himself to Susan's exaggerated response to pain and make it explicit that he was treating her because of conflicts reflected in such a response that made it especially difficult to make a diagnosis. Rather the therapist unwittingly got himself trapped into an either/or situation regarding etiology of the knee problem, when the issue was much broader than etiology alone.

As an aside, the psychiatrist was further impressed with Susan's exaggerated response to pain when a short time later he saw another girl with a painful knee. The attending pediatrician in the pediatric clinic sought psychiatric consultation after he determined on his physical examination that she suffered from no organic pathology. In this instance the psychatrist was impressed with the lack of evidence of an emotional disorder in this girl. Furthermore, falling back on his embarrassing experience of the past, he did discover some of the same physical signs that Susan had presented, though in this second girl there were no confusing histrionics with which to deal. The end result was that he did have her referred to the orthopedic clinic where the proper diagnosis was made and appropriate treatment given.

There is a definite need to emphasize that a diagnosis of emotional disorder should be made positively on the basis of demonstrable psychological factors and not be exclusively a negative diagnosis which is made simply because there is no other way to account for the child's symptoms at the moment. To rely essentially on exclusion of physical causes does certainly downgrade the psychiatric diagnostic process. However, the therapist also needs to be careful not to malign this diagnostic process by evidencing too ready a facility to give psychological explanations for anything and everything with which he is confronted.

PSYCHIATRIC EXAMINATION

As the therapist talks with the parents about their child and as he reads reports about him, he is bound to conjure up mental images of this child. It ordinarily is helpful to compare these images with the real child who then presents himself. It is fascinating to see, for example, that the "sweet little fun-loving" child as described by his mother is actually a snarling karate expert who is out to practice his skills in earnest. Or the therapist may be taken aback by the skinny little fragile-looking youngster after he had images that it must be quite a robust child who could immobilize a father who looks as though he were a candidate for lineman on a professional football team.

How does the therapist establish rapport that will help the child involve himself in the diagnostic process? Some may feel a need to be the Pied Piper of Hamelin after

whom children flock or a magician who wins the child's
favor with an alluring display of tricks. The first thing he
might remember is to avoid the temptation to resort to
gimmicks. Rather he may most effectively help establish
the necessary rapport if he approaches the child in a gen-
uinely sincere manner that conveys to him a spirit of empathy.
To hastily break the frightened young child from his mother
in the waiting room, for example, rather than first try to understand the nature of his fears would betray a lack of such
empathic spirit. Contrast this with the therapist who asks the
mother to accompany her trembling child to the examining
room and who then attempts to deal with the child's fears and
has the mother leave only after he has prepared the child for
her leaving.

With an older child it is possible that the therapist may
need to give other positive evidence that he is appreciative
and accepting of the child's feelings if he is to effect any
sort of adequate rapport. The following clinical vignette
illustrates one type of such concrete, positive proof.

> Jim was a fourteen-year-old boy who sat silently and was
> totally unresponsive in the therapist's office after he told the
> therapist that he would not talk because his mother had not
> told him that he had an appointment with a psychiatrist. The
> therapist told Jim that he could appreciate his anger towards
> his mother for her deception. Furthermore, he assured Jim
> that he was not approving of the mother's deception and that
> he had not been nor would he be party to it. When such
> expression of genuine concern for Jim's feelings and rights were
> to no avail in terms of making it easier for Jim to involve
> himself in the diagnostic session, the therapist saw Jim and his
> mother together. The therapist now expressed to both of them
> how he could well understand the mother's fear of telling Jim
> the truth about the appointment, as their relationship had so
> deteriorated, but he also shared with them his disapproval
> of lying to Jim in order to bring him to a psychiatrist. He
> suggested that they return home, that they try to discuss be-
> tween themselves the matter of psychiatric care, and that they
> return at a later date. To the mother's surprise Jim sub-
> sequently agreed to another appointment without protest. When
> Jim arrived for the second session, he provocatively stated,

"I've decided to talk. Aren't you glad?" The therapist needed to give hardly more than a smile of approval (and delight) before Jim spontaneously proceeded to talk about the turmoil in which he felt enmeshed at home.

The more usual way to establish rapport is much less dramatic, at least if the therapist finds it easy to talk with children, as he probably does or he would not be attracted to the field of child psychotherapy. Our discussion is beginning to sound more and more like a subterfuge for open acknowledgment that when it comes to specific advice about how to conduct a diagnostic session with a child, the going gets rough, as it is difficult to tell someone how to, in effect, establish a relationship. Fortunately, if one does quite automatically establish a relationship spontaneously, he does not need much in the way of specific directions.

There are, however, several questions about diagnostic interview technique that do commonly arise. There is many times the question of when and how to get at the child's presenting problem or problems. While a hard and fast rule is not feasible in this regard, the therapist ought at least to make it a point to talk with the child sometime during the first session about why he has come for diagnostic assessment. If the child himself does not raise the subject, it seems realistic enough that the therapist broach the subject. It seems unrealistic, but it does happen that a therapist completes the initial diagnostic session without mention ever being made of why the child came for examination. Such deliberate omission can hardly be reassuring to the child but in fact must leave him in a very anxious state, as he may wonder about the therapist's need for such guarded secrecy. If it looks as though it will be up to the therapist to raise the subject, when to do so is an important consideration. Many times it would seem reasonable for the therapist to discuss more general matters with the child, perhaps even to start with some light talk that comes to mind at the moment and in this manner give the child an opportunity "to get the lay of the land" before they talk about more anxiety-provoking matters. Such is the course many times when the child spontaneously talks about various and sundry matters, in the process of which he himself, at his own pace, probably with some unobtrusive nudges by the therapist, gently steers his way to the topic of why he was brought for examination.

There are times, however, when it may be helpful for the therapist to introduce the presenting problem at the beginning of the session. Such might be the case with the child who is very frightened about his visit and more specifically, frightened about what he imagines the therapist will think, say, and even do about his problems. He may figure that the best way to make sure that he does not end up talking about the problem is by not talking at all. In such an instance the therapist's matter-of-fact review of what he knows about the child's problems along with reassurance that he appreciates that the child "feels funny" about discussing the matter, if such anxiety is at all evident, may help to get across to the child that the therapist aims to understand and not to prosecute.

The going may get rough when conducting a session with the child who comes with behavioral problems for which he expects chastisement. Due to his feelings of guilt and on the basis of his past experiences with adults, he may figure that it is best to be noncommittal. The therapist in this instance may unwittingly initiate a "cat and mouse" game if he plays naive and asks the child to tell him about his problems but does not let him know that he has some awareness of these problems. The provocative youngster—and many with behavior problems do have this bent—may in turn attempt to "smoke out" the therapist in one way or another. He may, for example, sit back and refuse to talk while he does or does not taunt the therapist that he, the therapist, already knows about his problems so why should he, the patient, talk about them. The child may continue in this fashion until the therapist does acknowledge what he knows. Or the child may talk about his problems in such a sketchy manner or with such apparent distortions that the therapist is hard pressed not to jump in with the story as he heard it. In either of these two cited instances the therapist may find himself in a very awkward position if and when he does finally acknowledge what he has heard from the child's parents and others about his problems. Namely, rapport goes by the board as the child feels that he has proved what he had originally feared, i.e. that the therapist is out to trap him and in that regard is no different than everyone else he knows. It many times may be easy to avoid such fruitless struggles, which ordinarily are a reenactment of the child's everyday experiences, if the therapist openly though briefly tells the child what he knows about the problems at hand and then lets the child know that he is interested in hearing his view of the problems.

There is also the question regarding the extent to which the therapist ought to structure the diagnostic session in terms of asking questions and essentially steering the course of the session by his introduction of various topics to be covered. The therapist does need to appreciate that in order to understand the child's particular *modus operandi*, the manner in which he structures his world, he will need to give the child an opportunity to be reasonably spontaneous. To attain this goal, the therapist may need to encourage the inhibited, contain the hyperactive or the hyperaggressive child, or get back on course the rambler who avoids more meaningful exposition with his circumlocution. The aim then is not to totally relinquish the structuring of the diagnostic interview to the whims of the patient. The therapist must realize that there are different types of information that he needs to garner, some of which can be obtained only in a relatively unstructured session and some of which he will obtain only if he falls back on questions. Accordingly, to obtain information regarding the *modus operandi* of the child's psychological functioning, he needs to give the child relatively free rein. In order to gather certain bits of factual material, specific information about persons and events, he may need to ask the appropriate questions and in this manner structure the session.

There is yet another way in which the therapist might choose to structure the assessment interviews with a child. If it is a very young child or if the child appears to have problems on the basis of a reaction to some crisis event, the therapist might elect to create a play situation that parallels the event in the patient's real life. He then may ask the child to carry on play within this structured play setting. While mention of such use of play is made here, a fuller discussion of the subject is found in the chapter "Communicating with Children via Play."

Problems in Diagnostic Sessions

There are several pitfalls to avoid in dealing with a child already at this stage. There is the ever-present danger of treating him as an adult. The therapist may manifest this attitude in his choice of words and also in his unrealistic expectations of the child. For example, therapists commonly err in expecting too much self-awareness in a child, especially when it comes to awareness of affect. Much too often it may be forgotten that behavioral manifestations of an affect mask rather than are coupled with an awareness of the particular feelings.

There is also the danger of trying to seduce the child in an attempt to stimulate his spontaneity, be it to talk or be it to express feelings more freely. The ploy is simply for the therapist to align himself with the child's instinctual strivings in any of a number of ways. It might be that the therapist is too quick to voice approval of expression of feelings or gratification of wishes, be it a general statement of approval or an attempt to dismiss feelings of guilt or shame which the child has regarding some of his behavior. In any event the therapist comes out, in effect, on the side of the id. If the child is very much inhibited and saddled with severe superego restrictions, such alignment may actually frighten him away from the therapist even as he is already frightened away from his own feelings and wishes. If the child is impulse ridden and suffers personally and/or socially because of his transgressions or fantasied transgressions, he will understandably be suspicious of the person who says he wants to help even while he seems to encourage expression of that which already has him in a mess. There are also chances that he has his own repertory of superego bribes and that at some level he is aware of their inefficiency.

The therapist might elect to take the superego position, and such an approach with the child who has been referred because of his "bad" behavior is also ordinarily doomed to failure. Chances are that the child would not be at the therapist's office if he had been able to respond to reasonable superego pressures. To take a moralistic stance may put the therapist in line with the legion of other adults in the child's life who have futilely attempted to help him curtail his behavior by "preaching."

What is a reasonable position for the therapist to take? If he thinks in terms of id, ego, and superego positions—and there are advantages to such an orientation—the therapist sides with neither id strivings nor superego prohibitions but he attempts to take the position of ego functioning; he does not stand for impulse gratification of itself nor for prohibition of impulses of itself, but he stands for a self-mastery in which the child pays attention to his wishes and feelings and can gratify and express himself reasonably within a reality that he accurately perceives. Accordingly, if the therapist feels a need to prime the impulses of the in-hibited child, he will pay due respect to the child's superego forces and he will not ignore them or try to push them aside. For example, he might say to the inhibited child, "Though you feel funny about this, it would be good if you could let yourself feel the anger (or the excitement) and talk about it with me." With the impulse-ridden child he may lean toward the side of superego prohibitions, e.g. "You ought to feel bad about what you did to him" though he does not elect to censure the child for his instinctual expression and definitely not for his instinctual strivings. Rather again he tries to enlist the child's various ego functions, such as reality testing, self-observation, impulse control, to master impulses, as it is the development of such rather than emphasis on superego prohibitions that promotes ever greater self-mastery.

From another perspective it might be said that the child therapist especially needs to help the child patient distinguish between awareness of feelings and wishes and the expression of them. In effect, the therapist may need to help the child reorganize his conceptualizations and to counter his experiences at home. For example, in the child's mind, to get angry may mean to have a temper tantrum. The child may also very accurately perceive that when his mother says "Don't get mad!" she wants him to erase all feelings of anger. Accordingly, the therapist may very early let it be known very clearly that he himself distinguishes between the experience and awareness of a wish or feeling and its gratification or expression. He also makes it clear that he will not chastise the child for his particular feelings and wishes in the therapist's office. Furthermore, he invites the child to talk about them, but he definitely will expect a relatively reasonable expression of them in terms of behavior in the office. In this vein he will not hesitate to stop the child's physical attacks on him or to use reasonable restrictions to keep the walls from being torn down if the child himself cannot maintain a relatively reasonable decorum.

There is also danger that the therapist might feed into the child's pathological maneuvers in ways other than by an alignment with id strivings or superego prohibitions as noted above; he may respond to the child's manifest behavior and become involved in vicious cycles of interactional patterns in the manner in which the child ordinarily engages with those with whom he comes in contact. Accordingly, the therapist might respond in anger to the child's provocations, become mousy and submissive to the domineering child, or become unrealistically helpful and protective of the retiring child who by his very manner evokes such behavior in adults. As he pays attention to these characterological facets, the therapist also needs to be mindful of the various facets of any particular behavior if he is to appreciate more fully the "big picture." There are various levels of meaning in which behavior might be understood, as there are various tasks in which the behavior may be employed. For example, it is well for the therapist to appreciate that the provocateur is an angry child who needs to stir others to anger. However, he also ought to appreciate that the child's anger and angry displays are likely to be a defense against underlying fear and insecurity of which the child cannot let himself be aware.

Another problem area to consider is centered in the beginning therapist who may find himself confused and frustrated as he waits in vain for the child to talk. To wait may be especially difficult if the emotional distance between the adult therapist and child proves to be so great that he is unable to tune in on the child's behavioral messages. As this distance is reduced so that the therapist is more able to establish contact with the child and to tune in with him at the child's level, the lines of communication may be found to open more widely than was thought possible. In fact, he may even discover that the child is able to tell more about himself than the therapist ever dreamed a child could. It does appear that the lack of verbal communication at times is not due to the child's inability to express himself in that manner, but rather it may reflect unestablished lines of communication. In effect, it may be that the therapist acts as though he were about to communicate with another adult so that he puts the burden on the child to try to establish the contact with an adult, rather than he, the adult, establish the contact by means of calling into play his own childhood in his empathic overtures to the child.

Unestablished lines of communication for whatever reason also lead to the problem of "overdiagnosis" in the diagnostic assessment of either the child or his parents, though it is more likely to occur in the assessment of the child. The problem may manifest itself in one of two ways. The first form it takes, especially found in the assessment of the child, is that of a retreat into silence. It many times ends up that it is the silent child who is likely to receive a severe diagnosis. The second form involves a more complicated process. Herein the patient (child or parent) says or manifests something that the therapist interprets to be a sign of marked emotional disturbance. For example, the patient provocatively or otherwise says something that sounds very sadistic to the therapist. Rather than follow through on the statement to see what it meant regarding the patient, such as his need to shock, the therapist, most likely in his anxiety, tends to disengage himself even as he decides the patient must really be disturbed. From here, things may go from bad to worse. If the patient, for example, needs to provoke, he may unwittingly end up with wilder and wilder tales so that he really looks "out of it." In any event, in his anxiety the patient may look "looser and looser" while the therapist in his anxiety may be more and more ready to read whatever the patient says or does as a sign of severe emotional disturbance. What the therapist may fail to realize is that on the one hand he has provoked these manifestations from the patient by his own exaggerated reaction to the patient and that on the other hand in his anxiety-provoked premature assumptions that the patient is severely disturbed, he may have misinterpreted what the patient has said or done.

Rigidities built into the process of assessment, be it in a private practice or a clinic setting, may also pose problems in assessment of a child. The obvious antidote is flexibility. However, the problem may not be so readily averted if the therapist feels too much committed to a particular approach to diagnosis, such as a specified number and specified type of diagnostic sessions or particular diagnostic studies. If the therapist at the end of one session with the child and parents can answer the questions for which the family consulted him, why proceed with further diagnostic interviews and ancillary studies? If on the other hand the initial session points to a complicated problem in the child and his family, why should the therapist feel that he can and needs to understand the complexities thereof after one session or by individual interviews alone? Perhaps he needs to think of the additional pertinent information he might obtain through family interviews and/or other diagnostic studies.

Many times the first diagnostic interview will point to the nature of the problem but also to the fact that more examination is necessary in order to clarify the problem. With one child, one or several more interviews will be necessary. With another, a day care setting will help provide the opportunity for other professionals such as special education teachers and occupational therapists to help the therapist clarify his diagnostic impressions with their disciplined observations. Such may be the case, for example, in assessment of a child with academic and/or behavioral problems in a school setting, especially when there are obvious contradications between what is reported by the school and what the therapist observes clinically. To have teachers in the educational section of the mental health treatment facility interact with this boy in a classroom setting over two or three weeks may provide valuable insights into the problem at hand. With yet another child temporary placement of him outside the home in a hospital or residential treatment setting may be in order. Such placement might be helpful, for example, to ascertain more clearly the nature of the patient's symptomatology or if there is much question about how the child's problems fit in with the family's patterns of living. The child's symptoms may appear to be predominantly a reaction to a very difficult home situation, or conversely, the family setting may look just too intact to allow emergence of these particular symptoms. Separation of the child from the family for direct observation may be helpful under such circumstances. The use of hospitalization for such purposes is illustrated in the following clinical example.

Peter was a ten-year-old boy who had not been able to swallow solid foods over the previous three to four weeks. When seen for psychiatric evaluation he was very much guarded in his responses to the therapist and he came through as a boy who kept thoughts and feelings pretty much bottled up within himself. In the second diagnostic interview he did share with the therapist his fear that somebody might poison him. The therapist further learned from Peter that the problem with swallowing and the fear that he might be poisoned had their onset one noon while he was eating sausage at home.

Though Peter talked with the therapist about his symptoms over the next couple of weeks, they persisted unabated. The therapist was perplexed on two counts. On the one hand Peter did not look disturbed to the point of being delusional, as would be inferred from his fear of being poisoned. On the other hand it appeared logical to assume that if Peter was primarily a neurotic child, as he seemed to be, awareness of his irrational fear should have led to symptomatic improvement. Since the clinical picture continued in this confusing manner, it was decided that Peter should be admitted to the hospital for observation apart from his family.

In the hospital Peter's symptoms cleared within a few days after the hospital staff and other children in the hospital let it be known to Peter that they expected him to eat, as he just did not appear convincing in his protests that he could not swallow. It was further observed that he could eat without any apparent anxiety. From what was observed in the hospital along with a review of how his mother had handled his swallowing problems at home, it became more evident that Peter had obtained much secondary gain from his family as a result of his swallowing difficulties. It now seemed safe to say that the secondary gain was the chief factor to account for perpetuation of this symptom. Therefore, attempts were now made to help the parents deal with Peter in a more reasonable fashion as Peter continued in therapy on an outpatient basis.

Psychological Testing

When is psychological testing in order in the diagnostic assessment of a child? In some settings, psychological testing (IQ tests plus any of a number of projective tests) is part of the evaluation of all children who come for consultation. Unless such routine testing is employed without exception for research purposes or for training purposes, such testing would appear to be wasteful in terms of time and money because its usefulness on that basis is questionable at best. Furthermore, such routine testing might be relied upon to compensate for deficiences in clinical interviewing skills, and it is in this vein that beginning therapists may misuse psychological testing. In other instances undue reliance on psychological testing may reflect a skepticism about the validity of data garnered by interviewing. Unfortunately, in either instance there is likely to be a stunting in the development of clinical skills.

The value of psychological tests can best be appreciated if the therapist can realize that such testing is a valuable aid by which to acquire a fuller understanding of a patient, but it is not a substitute for clinical assessment. Their value is enhanced when the therapist goes to them to obtain answers to certain specific questions that he cannot answer satisfactorily in his clinical assessment. There are several areas in which psychological tests are especially valuable in this regard.

First, psychological testing may be invaluable in the assessment of mental retardation. Such tests can help gauge the current level of intellectual functioning and shed light on whether there is consistency or disparity among the various areas of intellectual functioning. They can also help to discriminate between the child's current level of functioning and his potential level. At the same time determination of mental retardation should not be made strictly on the basis of an IQ score. No problem ordinarily exists if a generalized lower IQ score goes along with a clinical picture of mental retardation. If, however, there is disparity between other data obtained in the clinical assessment and the IQ score, the therapist should not be quick to dismiss other data in favor of the IQ score lest he end up with an unrealistic diagnosis that may lead to unreasonable management of the child. The need to look further than to the IQ score when the possibility of mental retardation arises is seen in the following clinical example.

> Carol was a seven-year-old girl for whom the parents requested consultation, since on the basis of their own observations they could not believe that she was mentally retarded as they had been told. Carol had difficulty learning in school, and on psychological testing she had scored in the moderately retarded range.
>
> Clinically, Carol looked brighter, appeared more alert, and expressed herself in a manner that made her look to be of more average intelligence. Since the picture was confusing, not only was repeat psychological testing requested, but Carol was also observed in a day care setting over the next several weeks. Such further diagnostic assessment clarified the picture in the following way. It was now observed that Carol was an extremely negativistic girl whose resistance became more obvious when more age-appropriate demands were insisted upon. Her need to do battle definitely interfered with school performance, but it was also seen to interfere with her performance on psychological testing. Accordingly, plans for management of Carol now centered around a need to come to grips with Carol's disturbed object relationships.

Second, psychological testing may help on several counts to make a reasonable assessment of the child with learning problems. Intelligence tests shed light on the child's intellectual functioning and on his potential in this regard. There is other testing available to determine the various "perceptual-motor" problems that may interfere with the child's learning. Projective tests may help delineate the emotional constellations that may impede the child's ability to learn.

Third, psychological testing may prove helpful in establishment of a diagnosis of organic brain dysfunction. As such, testing can be a fine discriminator of mild organic brain dysfunction when it is important to make such determinations. The need for such determination ought to be prompted by a wish to understand more fully so as to plan more realistically for the child, but it ought not be based on the ill-founded assumption that a diagnosis of "organic brain dysfunction" and a recommendation for psychotherapy are mutually exclusive. Rather, if psychotherapy is in order, awareness of the organic dysfunction may help in arrival at reasonable decisions about educational programs and the possible use of medication in conjunction with psychotherapy.

Fourth, psychological testing may be invaluable in the assessment of the nonverbal child who shares little or nothing of his inner life with the examiner. It may be that either he lacks an awareness of himself or that he evidences an inability to communicate his awareness. In either event the examiner may end up nonplussed. It may become even more desirable for the therapist to obtain more data about the child's emotional functioning from psychological testing if this noncommunicative child exudes an aura of severe emotional disturbance about him.

DIAGNOSTIC FORMULATION

After he has obtained a description of the presenting problem along with a current picture of the child and his family through interviews with them so that he has an adequate cross-sectional view, and after he has acquainted himself thoroughly with the child's developmental history so as to have a longitudinal view, the therapist is then in a position to derive a diagnostic formulation. This formulation ought to provide a conceptual understanding of the child's problems through a plausible synthesis of the data which has been garnered. For such a synthesis to be plausible, the therapist needs to proceed in a orderly, logical fashion from the data at hand to successive degrees of abstraction. First there is a need for organization of the concrete data. Second, from this data the therapist might proceed to a "dynamic" explanation, that is, to outline the various components of personality functioning reflected in this data and to highlight the various intrapsychic and interpersonal processes that appear to generate the perceived behavior. Third, and only after he has integrated the material in the above fashion, the therapist may attempt to spell out the genetic factors (psychological and constitutional) that seem to have been involved in the original development of the current type and level of development. To proceed otherwise is likely to lead to a variety of errors. Primarily it may lead to much "dime store," amateur psychiatry in which there is nonproductive, sterile meandering into the land of the symbolic and the speculative rather than a more realistic emphasis on collection and reasonable organization of data, with close attention to observable, demonstrable data of which realistic formulations and reasonable therapy plans are born.

As earlier during assessment so now at the time of diagnostic formulation it would seem important that the therapist proceed as a physiologist and not as a pathologist. It is understandable that as a diagnostician the therapist is likely to find himself concentrating on the negative, the pathology, as he tries to delineate the problem more clearly. However, if he is to proceed from diagnostician to "problem-solver" he will also need to make himself aware of the positive aspects of the child's and family's functioning, especially since it is most likely that the potential for resolution of problems may lie in the positive. It seems safe to say also that undue emphasis on the negative and the pathological not only leads to unrealistically gloomy pictures but also leads to unreasonable recommendations. A more realistic formulation and a more reasonable therapy plan is ordinarily based on a realistic picture that includes not only the child's and family's unresolved conflicts but also their resolved conflicts, not only their vulnerabilities but also their strengths, not only their potential for symptom formation but also their potential for adequate functioning.

While the diagnostic formulation is capped with a diagnostic label, there probably is nothing less stimulating for a therapist who thinks in dynamic terms than for him to have to come up with such a label. With due respect for those entrusted with the frustrating task of arriving at a nomenclature for emotional problems of children, it needs to be remembered that labels tend to be meaningless unless accompanied by descriptive statements. Ordinarily such a statement ought to be embodied in the diagnostic formulation that precedes (or follows, if one is so inclined to arrange it) the diagnostic label. Without such a statement, labels, like other professional jargon, may tend to mask confusion and even profound ignorance.

III

COMMUNICATING WITH
CHILDREN VIA PLAY

THE CENTRAL ROLE of play in the development of modern child psychotherapy has been compared to the historical significance of hypnosis in adult psychiatry. Each has contributed considerably to the understanding of unconscious mental phenomena. It was the dawning appreciation of play as a vehicle of communication in therapy of children that spurred the development of child psychotherapy. Specifically, whereas Ferenczi did not appreciate the role of play and ended up feeling that children were unanalyzable because it was well-nigh impossible to have the child patient free-associate on the couch, Hug-Hellmuth described analysis of children through the medium of play. Since her day play has become the everyday tool of the child psychotherapist, and its nature has been conceptualized in many ways.

Play has been compared to fantasy in adults in its function as the bridge between the child and reality. Erikson proposes that the child's play is the infantile form of the human ability to deal with experience by creating model situations and to master reality by experimenting and planning." To him, "modern play therapy is based on the observation that a child made insecure by a secret hate against or fear of the natural protectors of his play in family and neighborhood seems able to use the protective sanction of an understanding adult to regain some play peace." He further goes on to note that "to play it out is the most natural self-healing measure a childhood affords." In this context the child's "playing it out" is equivalent to the adult's "talking it out."

Waelder discusses a number of characteristics of play which are as follows:

1. In play the child elaborates on material which he has experienced. "The incident experienced in reality may be given a different arrangement in play, but at all events the material is gathered from experience." In another sense, in play the child also elaborates his fantasies about real objects.

2. In play the child gratifies a desire for pleasure so that much of his play can be seen to be a manifestation of the pleasure principle. At the same time the child to a certain extent also plays because he derives pleasure from the activity itself.

3. Following the repetition compulsion which influences and drives him to reexperience, the child in play divides "excessive experiences" into small quantities that he can more easily assimilate. So play becomes "a method of constantly working over and, as it were, assimilating piecemeal an experience which was too large to be assimilated instantly at one swoop." In the process the child many times transforms a passive experience into one in which he is active, and in this manner he physically masters the impressions which were originally received in a merely passive way. For example, after a visit to his physician, the child may be found to play doctor, doing a physical examination, and giving "shots" to his sibling or friend.

4. In play "the child ventures to take over in a permissible way roles which are ordinarily prohibited by his education, and which later, once the superego has been formed, are also prohibited by his own superego." Waelder further quotes Kris, who said, "Play is a leave of absence from reality as well as from the superego."

Ekstein delineates three types of play in the therapy of children: (1) acting out, (2) play action that entails drama-type therapy sessions, and (3) play acting. He sees acting out as experimental recollection, play action as the slow replacement of impulsive and inappropriate action by a more advanced form of thinking, and play acting as an initial identification with a fantasied object in order to master the future experimentally. He further notes that the royal road to the unconscious of the child patient is play, which he sees as the child's best means for communication of his unconscious conflict. According to Anna Freud (1965), however, as free association seems "to liberate in the first instance the sexual fantasies of the patient, free action (as in play therapy) acts in a parallel way on the aggressive trends."

Play can be looked upon to serve two general functions for the child in psychotherapy: it is a motoric manner of self-expression and it is a motoric mode of communication. While either aspect can be emphasized at any particular time, both are invariably operative as the child plays in psychotherapy. Some child psychotherapists, however, have based their therapy on one or the other of these two functions of play. Fred Allen, for example, stressed the communicative aspect of play. Accordingly, he concentrated in therapy on the choice of the child's play, and he would not specifically consider the content of the child's play. In contrast, Melanie Klein, in her view that play is the equivalent of free association, emphasized the self-expressive aspects of play. However, Anna Freud (1965) cautions that play is not a valid substitute for free association. In his various expressions of play, the child does produce symbolic material, but without free association from the child it is difficult for the therapist to arrive at the latent content with any degree of certitude.

It might he said in summary that for purposes of therapy both the self-expressive and the communicative aspects of play must be appreciated. In this regard, play is to be viewed as any other behavior in the sense that it contains both a personal and an interpersonal component, i.e. the play reflects an attempt at gratification of drives (in the process the child projects his personality into the play), and the play becomes an important channel of interpersonal communication. In sessions with the child, the therapist needs to be aware of both the personal (intrapsychic, intrapersonal) and the interpersonal features of any behavioral expression. It can be anticipated that confusion may ensue when either feature is considered at the exclusion of the other. However, this is not to deny that it may be necessary to place emphasis on one or the other of these aspects according to what the therapist is aiming to accomplish in therapy or according to what is demanded in psychotherapy at the moment.

SETTING FOR THERAPY

If play is to be utilized effectively in psychotherapy, obviously there is need for a setting that will allow for reasonable expression and communication in play. To talk in terms of having a playroom may be misleading because of the possible connotations of "all play and no therapy." A conference in which an analyst was discussing the analysis of a preschool child comes to mind. During the course of the meeting, a psychiatrist who treated adults asked the analyst whether he used playthings with the child. This question caught the child analyst off guard as might the adult analyst be caught if someone asked him whether his adult patients talked to him during the course of analysis.

Generally in the psychotherapy of children, it is essential that the child be afforded opportunity for play, though the absolute need varies according to a given child at a given age. There is no doubt, however, that the process of psychotherapy can become severely hampered if opportunity for play is unavailable to the child patient in the preschool, early latency age group. How he is afforded this opportunity will vary according to dictates of space or preferences of therapist. The therapist either has playthings available in his office or he arranges a separate playroom away from his office. In the second instance the therapist might elect to tell his patient that they will use the office for "talk" sessions and will use the playroom for "play" sessions. To distinguish in this latter manner may have its advantages, but in the process the therapist can run the risk of belittling the importance of play in the child's psychotherapy, as chances are that he may unwittingly place undue emphasis on talk over play. In reality a combination of the two, engaged in simultaneously and not alternately, would seem to offer the most in psychotherapy of children.

If one were to spell out ideal settings, the therapist most likely would be talking in terms of a playroom setting for the pre-latency to early latency group of children and a regular office setting without playthings where he could see his adolescent patients. For the children who fall in the age range between the above-noted two groups, he would most likely find that an office setting with playthings available and an area in the office suitable for their use offers a setting conducive to psychotherapy. Though obvious, it may still be overlooked that the furnishings in the room in which there is to be play need to be appropriate for the particular play activities. Whereas board games will lend themselves to use in any type of setting, expressive materials like clay or paints necessitate prior planning. If the therapist is aiming for regressive play, the setting must be conducive to such play and must allow for such expression, or the child and his therapist may end up in one of two predicaments: either the child may get into the bind of being encouraged to regress by the very presence of play materials like paints and clay while suitable expression is unreasonably curtailed by the physical setting, or the mere setting may inhibit any sort of realistic regression which would be helpful in therapy.

Whereas the setting itself may offer considerable latitude in regards to regressive expression, the limits will most likely be determined by how comfortable the therapist can feel with the child's play at a particular moment. This is not to advocate greater or lesser tolerance on the part of the therapist in a particular setting but rather to remind him that he must anticipate and prepare for therapy with the child so as to avoid calamities or calamitous situations. For example, he will find that if he needs to be unduly concerned about keeping the room in one piece or the furnishings intact and clean, he will tend to become more a policeman than a therapist.

Similar considerations are in order when time comes for the therapist to procure playthings. In effect, he ought to make available playthings that will enhance attainment of his particular goals in therapy and that will be appropriate for the types of patients he treats. He can choose from among three general types of playthings: First are those which lend themselves to the child's use for self-expression. These include paper with crayons, pencils, and paints, and a blackboard and chalk. Also included are puppets and dolls along with playhouse furnishings, and cars and trucks. A second category would include items like sand, water, finger paints, clay and clay-like materials, all of which lend themselves to more regressive types of play. In the third group there are a whole variety of board games and cards that allow for competitive games between child and therapist. It may be necessary to remind at least the beginning therapist that in the procurement of playthings the aim ought not be to transform office or playroom into virtually a miniature toy store in which the child can entertain himself. Rather, as just previously noted, he ought to choose playthings according to what is appropriate for his particular physical setting and appropriate for the children he treats.

With the playthings available, how does the therapist proceed with the patient? There are two general options available to the therapist. First, he may elect to use "structured" or "directed" play (Hambidge). If he chooses this method, the therapist directs his patient to a given activity or he creates for the patient a given scene with the playthings at hand so as to get at certain material with the child. Such play may be especially helpful with a preschool child both for diagnostic purposes and for getting at particular conflicts with him. For example, the therapist may set the dolls as a family around a table and ask the child to engage in play with this family, as illustrated in the following clinical example.

> Sam was a three-year-old youngster with whom his mother was having a difficult time with his bowel training. Troubles began two months previously when the mother began insisting that Sam use a training chair six weeks after the birth of her second child. Sam responded with fecal retention that led to secondary soiling. Parental reassurances, insistence, and finally physical punishment only led to parental frustration. Unsuccessful pediatric interventions led to psychiatric consultation.
>
> During the course of the first session in the playroom the therapist arranged a doll family of father, mother, and two brothers, and he asked Sam to tell him about this family. In short order Sam had mother giving one of the boys a bath because "he got all dirty from coffee." It was then a short step from talk of "dirty from coffee" to talk of Sam's bowel problems at home. It emerged in this play context that Sam was extremely fearful of having bowel movements on the potty-chair. In subsequent sessions the therapist repeatedly structured play around the family in an attempt to get at the particulars of Sam's fears.

Second, there is the use of nondirective or unstructured play. Here the therapist leaves it to the patient to decide whether and how he will engage in play. Such use of play lends itself to expressive, exploratory psychotherapy in which the child is allowed to unfold his problems in play at his own pace and in the particular manner that suits him best.

To speak of play therapy as structured or unstructured may be misleading, especially if the unstructured variety sounds to smack of "just having fun" and not to have any therapeutic aim other than possibly catharsis. It might be more helpful and it actually is more accurate to think of both types of play as structured, but structured at different levels. Wheras the structured element of the first may be more self-evident, that of the second may seem more elusive. The structure of the second evolves and centers around the development of an atmosphere that allows the child to unfold his personality along with his problems in nondirected, spontaneous play.

In his role as empathic observer with the child, the therapist will need to try to understand the child's play in terms of the child's self-expressive and self-gratificatory wishes and in terms of the child's attempts to communicate specifically to the therapist in his play. At least the beginning therapist may need to be reminded that the child as patient does not play as he does by mere chance. Rather, undoubtedly his play is shaped by the presence of the therapist with whom the patient is always communicating overt and covert messages, unaware of this as he might be. So the therapist needs to be attuned to the child's play much as he would be attuned to the verbalizations and to the personality traits of a patient of any age. Specifically, the therapist needs to be attentive not only to the content of the communication but also to the transference implications of the patient's communications.

While in the introductory portion of this chapter the meaning of play was discussed from a general, theoretical standpoint, at this time it would be helpful to consider specifically how play serves as a means of self-expression in therapy. First, play lends itself to and does become a means of catharsis. The child discharges his impulses in the play situation, be it in annihilation of dolls or messing with finger paints and water. While there is an element of catharsis in all the child's play, this feature will be especially prominent in the generally inhibited child, regardless of more specific diagnosis, who begins to free up a bit in therapy, or in the more tightly controlled youngster who finds some regression tolerable to him within the safe confines of therapy sessions.

The previously inhibited or overly controlled youngster who enjoys the feelings of catharsis, as well as the impulse-ridden child who comes into therapy with actually or virtually no inhibitions, will many times traverse the same path in psychotherapy, i.e. each proceeds from disorganized, markedly regressed play in which discharge of drives is the primary consideration to play which is more organized and which involves more advanced ego functioning. Subsequently the degree of relative organization in play may wax and wane according to fluctuations in the child's ability to go beyond catharsis in play. A clinical example is seen in the following case:

> Paul, was a seven-year-old boy who was neurotically hyperactive. He began therapy by repeatedly "destroying" the the family dolls with blocks. He explained along the way that the different family members needed to be punished because they were bad, but it was obvious that no punishment would suffice. As he proceeded to destroy the family repeatedly, he virtually worked himself into a frenzy so that soon he was aimlessly throwing blocks around the room as he reveled in the noise he was making.
>
> This behavior continued for a number of sessions that were followed by a more organized and more controlled play as Paul responded to restrictions on his block tossing and interpretive comments on his play. Specifically, in his play he could now develop situations and elaborate themes without deterioration of his play into sheer destruction. However, intermittently there would be a return to his earlier play when he would become extremely anxious about something.

There is a second function of play in therapy, and this function might rightly be called the heart of play in therapy. Play in this regard is the means by which the child unfolds his personality, displaying the various levels of his personality functioniog along with his particular conflicts. It is then through play that the child patient can gain awareness of his own coping and defensive maneuvers along with awareness of that with which he struggles. Furthermore, as play initially aids the therapist in diagnostic assessment of the child, later it serves as a gauge for improvement in the child's functioning in terms of more mature personality functioning and resolution of conflicts. In effect, much as the child uses play in the natural process of development to master the task of growing up, so in therapy the child uses play to work out with his therapist specific problems which for one reason or another have not allowed for resolution in the child's daily play or in his other usual modes of coping with developmental tasks.

The first task may be to help the child become able to engage in play. In both his everyday life and in therapy, play may be just too threatening for him for any of a number of reasons. One child may be very much inhibited because he is fearful of drive expression in any form. Another child in his insecurity may be much too defensive to allow himself to project himself into play, puppet play or otherwise. An example of a child unable to engage in play follows.

> Susan was a ten-year-old borderline child who fought off any involvement with her therapist. During this period of time she would have nothing to do with him other than fight him either by provocative maneuvers or direct physical assaults on him. Such behavior continued for several months and receded only after the therapist physically restrained her when she attacked "for real." Restraining her without hurting her proved meaningful for her and she responded by becoming civil with him. She then did get to a point where she engaged in play with the therapist such as to become his secretary, and an officious, domineering one at that! In this play the therapist attempted at various times to introduce for discussion something related to Susan's conflicts. At times this approach was productive but at other times Sue would angrily accuse the therapist of talking about her. With acknowledgment that he now was on a hot subject, the therapist would get back onto more neutral subjects so as to maintain the play. With this approach the therapist found that over a period of time he was more and more able to help Susan deal with her conflicts in the displacement of play.

Another child who has trouble with play in therapy is the one who is unable to compete in any sort of reasonable fashion. He finds himself in trouble when he decides to play cards, checkers, or any of a variety of board games. A clinical example is as follows.

> Paul was a seven-year-old neurotically anxious boy. When he first played checkers in therapy, he would angrily strew the checkers all over the room when it was obvious that he was about to lose the game. From here he might even proceed to hit out at his therapist. After several sessions he did progress to a point where he would "grit his teeth" and bear a loss without falling apart. From there he proceeded to a point

where he would play another board game, one game after another compulsively in a very controlled manner.

As has been hinted already in the above-noted examples,
play becomes a ready bridge between the patient and his
therapist. In the process of play the child then goes on to reflect the nature of this object relationship with the therapist.
He may evidence an ability to relate in a comfortable, reasonable fashion. One child may need to be completely
helpless in play while another has to dominate the scene.
Others, in a competitive game, for example, may exhibit a
virtual sadomasochistic orientation. Commonly the child will
be found to interact with the therapist in play in a variety
of manners, depending upon his particular frame of mind
or emotional state at the moment and upon the progression
of therapy.

How a patient manifests this changing nature of his object relationships is seen in the following example.

> John, a six-year-old twin, was immature in many areas
> of functioning. There were many indications of persistent sym-
> biotic ties with his mother and much submission to his twin
> brother. John started out therapy with board games in which
> he initially acted confused and helpless so as to compel his
> therapist to tell him what to do and how to do it. When he
> won he would literally jump for joy. As therapy proceeded and
> the therapist did not give him all the assistance he invited in
> games, John became very independent in the game. He would
> make his moves without difficulty and gradually stopped asking
> for the infantile assistance he originally sought. Instead he now
> became markedly competitive and aggressive in games and
> played extremely well for his age. More and more, his gleeful-
> ness in winning also involved elements of "lording it over" the
> therapist and "rubbing it in."

While one child evidences the nature of his object relationships through his interaction with the therapist in a competitive game, another may evidence it in the content of his
play, such as in puppet play. For example, ten-year-old Bill
regularly demonstrated his sadomasochistic tendencies in his
puppet play. Affectionate gestures between the mother and

the father would regularly end in one biting the other. Playful gestures between the alligator and his master would repeatedly end with the alligator's devouring his master. (Bill would even add the sound effects of burping.)

Though there may be reason enough to advise the therapist to proceed with due caution in the use of games in therapy, there is no denying that games can be an invaluable aid in the establishment of a meaningful relationship. Such value is especially evident if games help the patient secure a comfortable position from which he can proceed to freer expression of therapeutically productive material.

An illustration of such progression is seen in the following clinical example.

Joseph, a seven-year-old, exceedingly inhibited, asthmatic younger, sat through early therapy sessions with his back to his therapist. He wriggled his body, whined, and cried angrily whenever his therapist tried to talk with him. When the therapist invited him to use any of the playthings available in the room, Joseph angrily insisted he would never avail himself of anything in the playroom. The therapist then decided to try to initiate something more with Joseph by bringing out the cards. He began to play solitaire but very explicitly told Joe he considered this play a mere interlude until Joe himself could openly engage in something—talk or play with him. After a short time Joseph began to look over his shoulder at his therapist and then got to ask him how the game of solitaire was played. Subsequently he did turn his chair around and gradually proceeded to initiate card and board games with the therapist. From there he proceeded to the blackboard where he drew various meaningful scenes, and he more and more talked about himself and his family.

Though games can be such a ready bridge between the patient and his therapist, there is no denying that the patient can also use the games as a powerful resistance to his involvement in a therapeutic fashion, especially when "insight-directed" therapy is attempted. In fact, the therapist may need to decide along the way whether games have lost their usefulness and have become a hindrance to therapy. A clinical example of how games do become a hindrance is seen in the therapy of Joan.

Joan was an eleven-year-old girl who evidenced many hysterical characteristics (marked dependence, coquettishness mixed with naiveté, and extensive use of denial and repression). To ever-increasing degrees Joan got herself lost in board games and card games during the course of her first year in therapy. Repeated confrontations by the therapist as to how she was using the games as a resistance fell on deaf ears, as Joan found it impossible to acknowledge that her behavior might be defensive. In this regard she acted much as when she would deny that her behavior at home or at school had varying types of meaning.

While the nature of the child's relationship with his therapist may seem more in the fore when the child engages in games, similarly the content of his play may dominate the scene when the child engages in more self-expressive play. In such play the child selects themes which give us a glimpse into his fantasy world and thus a glimpse into the nature of his particular conflicts. An illustrative example is seen in the following.

Larry was a nine-year-old neurotic boy who presented with problems of never having reasonably resolved the process of individuation and separation from mother. In his persistent attachment to his mother—an ambivalent one at that as such attachments are inclined to be—Larry evidenced much identification with his mother and had the resultant conflicts over sexual identity. The following excerpts from his therapy illustrate how in puppet play Larry portrayed these conflicts and how through puppet play he worked toward their resolution.

Larry had "Allie the Alligator from Alabama" (an alligator puppet) lead a campaign for men to sign a petition that all the men wear girdles and that all the women work outside the home. It turned out that one man refused to sign the petition and as a result he ended up in battle with the rest of the men. The campaign against the one dissenter continued for a couple of sessions. The cohesiveness of the men's bloc was then broken when Taddy (the frog puppet) decided to ask the therapist to shoot Allie the alligator, as Taddy decided he actually did not want to wear a girdle. The therapist in turn noted that Taddy's own hesitancy to shoot Allie was probably related to the mixed feelings he had about wearing girdles or not wearing them. Taddy responded by simply shooting Allie without any further ado. In turn the therapist observed how Taddy resolved his own problem with mixed feelings by shooting Allie. The therapist further ventured a guess that Taddy's mixed feelings would linger even though Allie was gone.

The third aspect of play is its role in communication in therapy. It is this feature of play in therapy that spells the difference between play in the child's everyday life and his play in therapy if development of greater awareness is the therapeutic aim. It is the therapist's concentration on the child's communication in play and his use of the child's play in this regard that may well decide whether the child stops at discharge of drives and catharsis or whether the child goes on to the development of greater awareness if and when such development is possible.

There is first the child's communication about himself. Since the child is not involved in play as one in isolation but in the presence of the therapist, the child's communication about himself will be influenced by his experience and awareness of the therapist's presence or by his real engagement with the therapist in a play situation. There is also the child's specific communication to and for the therapist through the medium of play, be it through the selection of his play, through the manner in which he plays, or through the content of the play itself. It is communication to the therapist as a "real" person to the extent that the therapist freely introduces himself into the child's life without specific attention to the manner in which he reciprocates to the child's wishes of him. It is also communication to the therapist as a "transference" person to the extent that the therapist introduces himself as little as possible into the child's life as he emphasizes a particular type of reciprocation to the child's wishes of him, i.e. he deemphasizes gratification of the child's wishes of him as much as is reasonably possible while he emphasizes the need for the two of them to examine their interchange for purposes of ever greater awareness.

THERAPEUTIC MANAGEMENT OF PLAY

If it is accepted that communication is such a vital element in the child's play in therapy, the therapist needs to be, above all else, an observer of the child's play, regardless of the extent to which he decides to involve himself actively in the child's play. He may then involve himself primarily as a nonparticipant observer or as a participant observer. In the usual psychotherapy of children he may very likely find that during the course of therapy with a given child, fluctuation between these two approaches toward play will be the rule rather than the exception. Put another way, the therapist's effectiveness will most likely be dependent on his ability to choose options rather than by his commitment to one or the other degree of involvement in the child's play.

As a nonparticipant observer the therapist elects not to be actively involved in the child's play. It should be noted that "nonparticipant" refers to the therapist's lack of active involvement since it needs to be remembered that the therapist will be involved regardless of what he does. His mere presence involves him, whether or not he wishes to be involved. In effect, the therapist lets the child know that he will involve himself primarily as an observer while he himself recognizes that the child may have other roles in mind for him, be it critic, judge, adversary, or accomplice, depending upon what the child's fancy dictates at the moment.

When he adopts the role of the nonparticipant observer, the therapist will avoid any competitive games. If the child will attempt to involve him in something like puppet play, the therapist may passively take one of the puppets but only to dramatize the script which is written by the patient, introducing himself personally into the performance to a negligible extent. If the child invites his therapist to join with him in acting out a scene, the therapist might elect to do something akin to what was done in the following clinical example. When Paul, an eight-year-old-neurotic youngster, decided that he would lead an expedition to kill the President of the United States, he offered his therapist a gun and invited him to join in the conspiracy. Rather than accept this invitation the therapist suggested that he join the expedition as newspaper reporter.

When the therapist elects to be a participant observer he

can choose to be one at any of several levels. First, he may passively assume the role given to him by the patient and closely follow the script written by the patient. In this way he attempts to introduce himself only negligibly into the play situation.

Second, the therapist may assume the role assigned to him by the patient but then he may write his own script even while he concentrates primarily on reacting to or elaborating on what the patient introduces. This method lends itself to introduction of material from the "real life" experiences of child patients who are especially inhibited or guarded about certain aspects of their lives. An example of such an approach was cited earlier from the therapy of Susan who played that she was her therapist's secretary. Her therapist in turn elected to introduce material related to reports he had received about her interactions with staff and other patients in the hospital in which she was being treated.

Third, the therapist himself may take the initiative in play therapy. He might do so, for example, by encouraging the child to avail himself of a particular mode of communicative play. With this in mind, the therapist might take a toy telephone and begin to "phone" the patient to whom he has offered another telephone. Or the therapist might begin to talk to a puppet who he makes believe is aware of the patient or whom he "directs" to communicate with the child patient. An example of such use of play is seen in the following clinical example.

> Mary was a nine-year-old neurotically inhibited girl. Mary became fascinated with the frog puppet but she merely fingered it cautiously while she proceeded with care as was so characteristic of her. The therapist took this opportunity to talk with the puppet, asking it its name and where it had been. Mary hesitated nervously as though she did not know what to do with the puppet. Still trying to get something going with Mary through the puppet, the therapist suggested that maybe the puppet would whisper to her, as he might be hesitant to talk directly to the therapist. Mary's face brightened, as she liked this idea. She now began to play that the frog was whispering to her information that she in turn conveyed to her therapist.

When the therapist himself initiates play with the inhibited child he may accomplish several things. Not only may
he help the child communicate more freely, but in the manner of his approach the therapist may also encourage or
even initiate the sort of regression that will be so useful in
the therapy of the child. Specifically, the therapist not only
invites the child to play "make-believe" but shows him how
it can be done.

As a fourth alternative, the therapist may elect to be a
participant observer in a competitive game. The therapist
again has the option to allow the child to initiate the move to
play a game or he himself may suggest that they play a game.
It is true that in such interchange the therapist can readily become more of a "real" figure than a "transference" one.
It is also true that the outcome in this regard will to a great
extent depend upon the game he plays and upon the manner
in which he approaches the game. Above all, reason also
ought to dictate choice of games. Not only should the game
be age-appropriate but it should also be of a variety that
does not militate against therapy. A game like chess or
Monopoly, which requires an inordinate amount of concentration, skill, or time, does not lend itself well to use in therapy. Generally a more strictly "chance" game, for example
a board game that requires little skill, since the players alternately draw cards that direct a player how to proceed,
need not restrict therapy to strictly the relationship variety.
Such a game can still be used in therapy geared primarily
toward the development of greater awareness if the therapist
approaches the game in a realistic fashion, i.e. if he plays in
a reasonably competitive fashion so that he avails himself
of the usual opportunities to win that are afforded to him in
the game. To deviate from such an approach, such as to play
a "cutthroat" game or to throw the game so that the patient
wins, will ruin any opportunity to utilize the game for therapeutic purposes.

If the game does require some degree of skill, such as
checkers or some card games, reason might dictate that the
therapist make allowances for the patient because of the dis-

parity in skill between the two. Rather than make poor moves that actually destroy the game, the therapist might more reasonably balance the game by giving the patient a handicap. (If the child is the more skillful player, the therapist ought to be able to find cogent reasons why further play of this game is antitherapeutic!) A word of caution: It is not unusual to find that the awarding of handicaps is met with objections from the child who is in distress in his object relationships as emotionally disturbed children are wont to be. The therapist will find that the child is virtually as anxious about winning as he is about losing, for he is uncomfortable with either result.

From his established position of observer, nonparticipant or participant, the therapist can then proceed into an interpretive role. The task of interpretation, which involves a many-stepped process (discussed in the following chapter), is a unique one in the psychotherapy of children because the therapist has one of two ways to proceed with the play material, except when it comes to competitive games: (1) he has the option to handle the child's play productions strictly in displacement—he can talk to or about the play characters in "make-believe" fashion—or (2) he can elect to extrapolate from the play into the real life situation of the child. In the so-called "uncovering" variety of therapy, the more usual procedure would be to remain in the play situation as much as possible, to make all interventions within the context of displacement, to even remain there throughout therapy unless the patient turns from it to his own life situation. If and when the patient does turn from the play to his own life situation, the therapist needs to decide whether it is preferable to deal with the "real life" events or to encourage the patient to return to the play, especially if he may have retreated from it in his anxiety. In effect, the therapist needs to determine whether further regression into fantasy at the moment is desirable and therefore to be encouraged, or whether it would be preferable to discourage such regression and deal with the reality that the patient now introduces.

To have a child prematurely return to real experiences in his life appears to be a more frequent technical error than to foster his further elaborations in play. The therapist may too quickly become engrossed in the symbolic equivalents of play. Since he feels that he very clearly understands the meaning of the child's play, he may feel compelled to interpret so as to share his insights with the child. Unfortunately, such interpretations that are directed to the child's "real life" experiences prematurely and without sufficient preparation much too often prove to be wet blankets on the child's productions and offer nothing but intellectualized insights at best.

PROBLEMS IN PLAY THERAPY

When he deals with the child's play, the therapist is likely to find himself confronted with at least one of a number of problems that need to be resolved. Foremost on the list is the problem of setting limits in play without at the same time unduly inhibiting the child's play. Since the usual aim is for a reasonable expression of feeling and fantasy that can lend itself to development of greater awareness, setting of limits will center around the determinations of "ego controlled regression" or "regression in the service of the ego", i.e. the child is allowed to continue freely in spontaneous play to the extent that it allows for development of greater awareness, and he is curtailed in his play when play becomes nothing more than drive discharge—play simply for the sake of play, and regression for the sake of regression. It is also assumed here that brakes are applied before the child physically hurts himself and/or the therapist, or before he destroys the environs.

It obviously is not always easy to determine where to draw the line, where and when to set limits in play. The task may be easier if the therapist constantly views the child's play in terms of ego functioning. The aim in play, as in all of psychotherapy, is to engage the child's ego functioning or to help the child develop the level of ego functioning that will allow for the involvement of the child in a therapeutic alliance that ordinarily calls for the child to reflect on what he is doing. In this context, and as already alluded to above, if observation and reflection are tossed by the board as the child becomes utterly involved in the activities of play, the child is brought back to a reflective position, and play is limited as deemed necessary to establish the desired therapeutic involvement. On the other hand, when lack of impulse control or disturbed reality testing, for example, leads to extremes in play, the therapist may set limits on the child's play by mobilization of more adequate impulse control or reality testing that the child lacks.

The role the therapist takes in reference to the child's play may also pose problems that need to be taken into account. A great danger in this regard is that the therapist unwittingly may give up his role of therapist to become the patient's playmate. Chances are that he will become a very submissive one at that. In any event, therapy is then reduced to practically no more than an opportunity for instinctual gratification for the patient and/or the therapist. This problem may manifest itself in any of several ways. It may, for example, take the form of playing games endlessly even though they lead nowhere. In this case the therapist may rationalize that he does not want to inhibit the patient, whereas in reality he may be avoiding the need to make a determination about the reasonable course to take in therapy. At any given moment in therapy, to curtail play may be the most reasonable course to follow.

Problems around the role to be assumed by the therapist also arise when the therapist blindly carries out whatever the child dicates him to do in play, not taking into consideration what impact his participation has on the patient. This consideration becomes especially important the more the emphasis in therapy is on the development of greater awareness or when the child manifests a significant disturbance in reality testing. For example, the therapist will need to consider the impact of his repeatedly playing a game of "cops and robbers" with the child who time and again provocatively attempts to engage in a sadomasochistic relationship with the therapist and in the process eludes engagement in uncovering therapy. This play might further become inadvisable because the child may not merely assume a role but for all practical purposes may lose his own sense of identity in this play.

The therapist who becomes the submissive playmate of the child may also run the risk of physically falling to the mercy of the child. For example, there is the therapist who gets himself securely tied to a chair in "playful" gangland fashion only to find himself left to the mercy of his captor. In another instance the therapist finds himself locked out of his office by his "playful" captor who fleeced him of his keys.

How should the therapist be expected to act with his patient in the play situation? The therapist who maintains the tone of therapy is the one who maintains a realistically secure therapist-patient relationship. As therapist he may assume any of a variety of roles in play, be it an active or a passive role, a dependent one, or one in which he is the master. In any event both he and the patient realize that he assumes a particular role by choice. Furthermore, whereas the patient may find it difficult to disentangle himself from a particular role, the reasonable therapist can return to his *real* position of therapist according to the progress of therapy. Whereas at one moment it may be desirable for him to remain a character in play, at another time he might more reasonably return to his more strictly observing and interpretive roles. At still another time in therapy he will need to switch from his particular role in play to setting limits in play, such as when the child is "carried away" by the play.

There are several reasons why a therapist may find it difficult to approach play in such a flexible manner. First, it may be that he attempts to bribe his patient by being "the nice guy" who tries to win him over by being his "playful buddy." Second, there may be various countertransference problems that compel the therapist to overly identify with this particular patient so that he finds it difficult to use play in any sort of realistic fashion. Such a therapist may especially find himself in trouble when it becomes a matter of whether or not to set limits to the particular play. Third, the therapist may need to become very actively involved in play in order to deal with or avoid the anxiety he experiences when he is forced to be passive. Such a therapist might actively encourage games or actively intrude himself into the child's play because he cannot tolerate to sit back passively to listen to the child or to observe him as he draws, paints, or plays with blocks.

How to respond to a child who cheats in a game poses another problem that will confront the therapist at one time or another in play therapy. To reprimand the child is hardly therapeutic, and to ignore the fact that he cheated is equally unrealistic. What can the therapist do and still remain therapeutic? He can start out from his position of observer to confront the child with the obvious and proceed to interpret to the child what he does with his cheating. It may be that the child is looking for the therapist to be his "conscience" or to be the "policeman." In another instance the child may be attempting to see whether the therapist is allied to superego or id, i.e., if the therapist says anything at all, the patient may take the comments as chastisement, and if the therapist says nothing, the child may see him as identified with wanton gratification of wishes. If a child persists in cheating in spite of the therapist's confrontations and interpretive remarks, the therapist may have no choice but to not play, as there is no way to go with games at that point.

Subtler forms of cheating to which therapists in their natural gullibility as therapists are prone to be more vulnerable are posed by the child who is constantly changing the rules. The therapist in his wish to avoid criticism of the patient may rationalize these "innovations" in one way or another. When it is obvious cheating, the therapist can respond along the guidelines noted above according to what the child is communicating in this behavior. With such a patient the therapist can further emphasize to the child that he primarily wishes to assume a reasonable position by letting the child know that in the future he will be ready to entertain rule changes before they begin a game. A further word of caution regarding rule changes is needed. Rather than signs of creativity, elaborate modifications of rules more often than not prove to be manifestations of very prosaic resistance. In effect, the therapist and the patient will need to remain so much preoccupied with the game and all its modifications that the play loses its therapeutic usefulness.

How about the child who bends the rules in favor of the therapist? Again the therapist may be hamstrung but for different reasons. To make any comments may seem downright nasty since the child is being so "generous." Not to to say anything conveys the dubious message, "It's okay for you to cheat if the cheating is for my benefit." As with anything else in therapy, the therapist once again needs to attempt to get at the meaning of this behavior even while he lets the patient know that the game is hardly a game unless they both abide by the rules.

A last problem in dealing with the child's play centers around whether the therapist should respond to the content of the play or to the child's covert communications to the therapist. A common error, that of responding primarily to the content of the play, is illustrated in the following clinical example.

Joe was a hyperactive, neurotic eight-year-old youngster who was showing his true form in therapy as he made a shambles of the playhouse and its contents while the therapist sat back passively. Finally Joe settled on the mother doll and began manhandling her. The therapist dealt with this behavior by merely wondering what the boy in play had against his mother. Later in supervision it was pointed out to the therapist how the patient's behavior with the mother doll seemed to have other implications. The material pointed to Joe's concern of "What do I have to do to get a rise out of this guy? Maybe showing him I am a mother-killer will finally get him to realize how bad I really am!"

The point is that the child's play as well as his verbal productions and all other behavior in therapy needs always to be assessed for intrapsychic meaning and for interpersonal messages. It then becomes a matter of clinical judgment at the moment as to which of the two aspects ought to be handled, if the therapist feels it necessary to respond at all.

IV

THE STRATEGY OF CHILD PSYCHOTHERAPY

To ADVISE A THERAPIST on how to conduct psychotherapy with his particular child patient may in itself be a difficult task in the usual supervision that is commonly found to be part of the training of psychotherapists. To attempt to advise in any sort of meaningful fashion how to generally conduct psychotherapy may sound to be a most formidable task. Therefore, it is easy enough to discuss questions about the manner of approach in psychotherapy by emphasizing the singularity of psychotherapy with a given patient and to accuse the one who asks for more specifics of looking for recipes.

There is the danger that discussion of therapeutic maneuvers might end up sounding as though the author believed that a therapist's contributions can be reduced to simple formulas. However, the danger is minimized and the discussion is legitimate enough if it is done within the context of explaining the rationale for a particular action. To discuss the strategy of psychotherapy in this context is to emphasize that psychotherapy needs to be based on a systematic, organized understanding of the child and his family as well as on such understanding of the process of psychotherapy. Without such understanding it is difficult to envision any sort of reasonable approach to psychotherapy. On the other hand, this is not to say that the therapist is to become a cold, calculating deliberator who loses his spontaneity with patients. Ideally, what he does (or what he does not do) in therapy is based on his intuitive awareness at the moment and is guided by his understanding of the child and of the therapeutic process. He acts on the basis of what he sees, hears, and feels at the moment and also on the basis of what he decides the child needs in therapy at the moment and/or what is needed to keep the therapeutic process progressing in a reasonable fashion.

There are three facets to this strategy of psychotherapy that need to be taken into account in any consideration of therapeutic maneuver. First, there is the matter of what to do; this gets at the very nature of the therapist's activity in psychotherapy. Second, there is the matter of *why*; this gets at the reasons for the therapist's particular behavior at a given moment and touches on the whole matter of timing, which may be so crucial in any type of intervention. Third, there is the matter of *how*; this gets at the specifics regarding the manner of execution of therapeutic plans.

THE NATURE OF INTERVENTIONS

Though it may be difficult and even well-nigh impossible to tell a therapist what to do at any particular time in therapy with any particular child, one can categorize the variety of options that are available to the therapist in his work. The types of therapeutic interventions might be viewed on a continuum that encompasses the broad scope of activity by the therapist—the total spectrum of his activity. This activity ranges from attempts to obtain a clearer picture of the child and his problems to attempts to help the child integrate and utilize the newly acquired information about himself.

Starting on the information-gathering side, the simplest way to intervene is to ask the child questions about what he says or does so as to get a clearer picture of what the child is presenting. The therapist may then go on to further clarify the picture by recapitulation and reorganization of the child's productions so as to establish temporal sequence and logical order. These steps in effect pave the way for confrontation, i.e. the bid to engage the child in an active examination of the material at hand so that the child might get at the implications of what he says and does. Put another way, in his confrontation, the therapist asks the child to step back to take a look at the picture he himself has just drawn. At this stage, however, the emphasis remains on the expressed or the implied feelings and motivations as the therapist remains with the material that the patient presents and does not attempt to introduce new dimensions such as unexpressed motivations of which the patient may remain unaware. An illustration of the therapist's interventions in the above fashion is seen in the following clinical example.

> Tom, a ten-year-old boy, showed his therapist the "wounds" on his hand as he explained in a matter-of-fact fashion that his mother had scratched him during a concert the previous afternoon because he was talking with his younger brother. On further questioning it was clarified that Tom's mother must have been beyond herself with fury because he had been fooling around not only during the concert but during an earlier church service, disregarding her many admonitions and reprimands. As the picture was drawn out still further it was learned that on the way home from the concert Tom had chided his mother, "Are you glad now that you scratched me? Why do you tell Sue (his sister) she can't scratch people when you yourself scratch?"
>
> After the therapist obtained the "big picture" by asking Tom for specifics about what had happened, the therapist in effect started with the end result and tried to work his way back. Accordingly, he first confronted Tom with the observation that he had acted as though he were trying to make his mother feel guilty on the way home from the concert. When Tom acknowledged he had acted in that fashion, the therapist went on to note that in this manner he had distracted himself from painful consideration of his earlier interaction with his mother, i.e. how extremely provocative he must have been with her all afternoon (as he was regularly wont to be with his parents).

When the confrontation is established—when the patient acknowledges that he and the therapist are aware of the same bit of reality—then and only then is the ground set to make the next step, i.e. to interpret something beyond the patient's conscious awareness. Or, with the *what* established, the patient can be helped to understand *why* he acted as he did on the basis of unconscious functioning or unconscious motivation. While the above may sound very elementary and be passed over lightly because it amounts to "nothing more than common sense," such elementary logic can be easily forgotten in therapy. Accordingly, it is not unusual to find that a therapist attempts to get at the why's and wherefore's with a patient before he and the patient ever agree on what the patient has said or done or on how the patient feels. Such a technical error (one of the most frequent in psychotherapy) is especially found when the therapist puts his emphasis on the bestowal of insights. As might be expected, such a therapist stands the risk of reducing psychotherapy to a series of intellectualized discussions.

In the above-cited example, the therapist went on to interpret to Tom that he had attempted to make his mother feel guilty in order that he himself might avoid feeling guilty. From this base the therapist proceeded to expand on how Tom must have protected himself from as yet undetermined anxiety during the course of the afternoon by his constant disruptive and provocative behavior. Herein the therapist was falling back on his awareness that Tom was a neurotic youngster who regularly defended himself from affect by this very same behavior.

When he elects to interpret, the therapist does attempt to add another dimension to what the child says or does. Namely, he attempts to help the child become aware of motivations that lie beyond his awareness. Be the content of the interpretation *defense* and *affect* as in the above clinical vignette, or be it *impulse* and *conflict* in another instance, the common denominator in interpretation is the fact that the particular content does lie beyond the child's conscious awareness. To say that the content lies beyond conscious awareness still does leave a great deal of latitude so that some qualifications are in order. The main thing is that the therapist ought not feel he has license to plumb the depths with utter abandon. Ideally it is unconscious material that might be said to be at a preconscious level, i.e. material of which the patient has some difficulty becoming aware but from which many of the repressive forces have been removed with the help of previous confrontations and interpretations. While the aim of interpretation is to make the patient conscious of unconscious material, ordinarily the most meaningful interpretations center around preconscious material, as the interpretation is but the last step, the final assist, in the attainment of greater awareness. Ordinarily the therapist will find that such concerns about the level of awareness at which to intervene pose no problem as long as he follows along with the material as presented by the patient. He then finds himself encouraging a progressive expansion of the child's awareness. In the process he will find that it is not for him to reach for content but rather to help the child unwrap the content.

Beyond interpretation on this continuum of interventions lies education. Herein are included all attempts to expand personality functioning other than by removal of emotional complexes that interfere with ever greater development of personality functioning. Educational interventions would then include the imparting of new knowledge and attempts to have the patient exercise certain personality functions such as impulse control and critical judgment. It might be said that psychotherapy ordinarily is geared toward making the child more responsive to the usual educational forces to which children are exposed formally and informally. As a corollary it might also be said that education itself is not the aim of psychotherapy. Yet in the psychotherapy of children the line between psychotherapy and education does become especially blurred, and education does become an important ingredient in the psychotherapeutic process. For example, there may be times in the psychotherapy of children when education, such as giving the child some needed information, might be in order in place of an interpretation. Such would be the case when further clarification of a problem reveals that the child's problem at the moment is related to lack of exposure to such knowledge rather than related to emotional blocks or complexes.

In a sense the child psychotherapist is regularly forced to make a decision between confrontation-interpretation and education. This is especially the case when the child comes with a multitude of questions about relevant and irrelevant matters as children are wont to do. In effect, he then needs to choose between dealing with the inquisitive child as defensively curious or just plain old curious. Or he may need to decide whether the child is actually uninformed (e.g. about sexual matters) because of lack of exposure to knowledge or whether the child has remained consciously uninformed, though exposed to knowledge, because of interferences to his assimilation of knowledge. Even though the former may be the case, i.e. a true lack of exposure, it is important that the therapist watch lest he find that he has assumed the role of educator—parent or teacher—and in the process has given up his role of therapist. From the child's side, "being simply curious" can be a powerful resistance to therapy. The therapist can best avoid the pitfalls laid by the "curious" child if he reserves the bulk of education in therapy sessions to educating the child about the therapeutic process itself.

On the continuum beyond education but yet much akin to it are *advising, counselling,* and *directing.* Here, too, as in educational attempts, such activity by the therapist ought to be restricted primarily to advice, counsel, or direction in reference to the therapeutic process itself. It may be a matter of curtailing certain activities in which the child engages, e.g. assaultive behavior or regression for the sake of regression, in order to keep therapy moving. An even more direct intervention, however, ought to be employed only after it is proved that lesser interventions which are geared more toward mobilization of autonomous personality functioning are to no avail. For example, refusal to engage any further in board games would be in order after interpretation of the defensiveness of such activity proved to be ineffective in terms of helping the child make more reasonable use of such activity. In yet another instance the therapist may need to resort to what might be considered to be the most drastic therapeutic intervention, i.e. physical restraint. Again the therapist might reasonably be expected to physically restrain the assaultive or destructive child only after lesser means of mobilizing his own impulse control, e.g. interpretive comments regarding the defensiveness of his behavior, prove to be ineffective.

An illustration of how a therapist may need to employ a wide range of interventions and how anticipation of behavior can result in more effective use of lesser interventions is seen in the following clinical example.

Pat was an eight-year-old hyperactive child who used motoric activity as a powerful defense against painful affect. Such activity would at times culminate in assaultive attacks against his therapist. As a result, many times during the second year of therapy the therapist needed to hold Pat securely when negative transference feelings consistently led to assaultive behavior. At such times it was impossible to get Pat to control himself through awareness of affect and through more reasonable expression of affect. Though such restraint eventually helped to diminish the occurrence of Pat's assaultive outbursts, there still were times when he could readily revert to such behavior. However, at the same time the therapist more and more took note of the very early signs of inner turmoil, e.g. preoccupied look, aimless wandering from object to object, tossing objects off the play table early in the session as though he were clearing it for his use. The therapist more and more confronted Pat with his behavior at an earlier stage in attempts to get at underlying affect. Intermittently the therapist would need to curtail behavior like playing games with the room darkened or using water to the extent that he was about ready to flood the place, because such behavior was but a short prelude to uncontrolled behavior which might easily lead to physical attacks against the therapist.

Furthermost on this continuum of interventions is manipulation—to "control or modify the action by management." Actually, such intervention is much akin to the directing noted above. However, in psychotherapy of children it extends over into dealing with the family in a manner conducive to modifying or realigning forces among the various members so as to facilitate the resolution of problems and to enhance "normal" development.

A word more about this continuum of interventions: No value judgment ought to be attached to any intervention of itself on this continuum. Each is valid and valuable in its own right. One intervention is not to be considered superior to another in its own right. It does need to be remembered, however, that the emphasis on particular types of interventions is bound to shape the nature of the therapeutic process. The more the therapist stays to the side of confrontation-interpretation, the more he allows for examination of another dimension in the child's functioning, i.e. unconscious emotional complexes. The more he leans toward the education-counselling side, the more he relies on dealing with the child in terms of conscious personality functioning and conscious motivation. In another sense, the former lends itself to personality development by means of removal of emotional impediments, while the latter lends itself to development via bolstering and nurturing of established personality functioning.

The course to follow, however, ought not be dictated by the bias of the therapist but rather by the nature of the child's difficulties and by his particular needs. Generally speaking, one might say that paradoxically the child at either extreme, be he fairly intact and relatively free of neurotic traits in his personality functioning or be he extremely disturbed with gross defects in personality functioning, will more likely be responsive to the educative-counselling type of interventions, though in different ways. In contrast, the child with neurotic traits and neurotic conflicts may be more effectively involved in therapy with the emphasis on confrontation-interpretation.

THE SUBSTANCE OF INTERVENTIONS

Another aspect of intervention to consider regarding the *what* involves the substance of the intervention. This falls into two general categories that include the content of the child's productions and the various aspects of the therapeutic relationship, i.e. the reality-based and transference-based aspects. There are several factors to consider when it comes to the content of an intervention. Foremost among these is the patient's level of awareness of this content. In effect, the therapist needs to keep in mind that he is to start with material of which the patient is aware and expand from there as indicated, i.e. he is to deal with manifest content first and only then move on to latent meanings. Accordingly, he starts with what the patient says or does and has the patient observe this content or has substantial evidence that the patient has observed it. If the patient cannot perceive the blatantly obvious, it would be gratuitous to expect the patient to be open for consideration of hidden aspects. For example, if the patient at the moment cannot acknowledge his obvious tearfulness or if he cannot detect the sarcastic ring in his comment, it would be folly for the therapist to expect the child to be receptive to consideration of underlying affect in either instance. Rather the therapist will need to deal with the child's use of denial and resultant lack of awareness before he can have the patient examine the content. Chances are that the therapist will need to switch over to consideration of the transference implications of these defensive maneuvers before he returns to the content.

What is the substance of the manifest content? Essentially this content will include behavior and affect along with the child's verbal productions. However, a word of caution regarding affect must be added. More than might be generally expected, the child may be quite oblivious of affect, not merely defensively but due to the very fact that a child ordinarily may just not be reflective on how he is feeling. This fact needs to be kept in mind even while the therapist is attuned to the defensive nature of behavior in the "action-oriented" child with behavior problems and the isolation of affect evident in the obsessional child. After he deals with such manifest content the therapist ordinarily can, if need be, consider defenses and resistances of which the child is relatively unaware. If the therapist then deals with these, he does so essentially to pave the way for ever greater awareness through a greater array of manifest content.

As the therapist proceeds in the above stepwise fashion from the *manifest behavior* and *affect* to *defenses* and *resistances*, he then arrives in the position where he is able to deal with *impulse* and *conflict*. A common technical error in therapy is committed by the therapist who deals with impulses before he deals with the patient's defenses against these impulses. He in effect rides over defenses by the use of so-called "id interpretations" rather than helps the patient work through these defenses. He is likely to generate a "hypertrophy" of the defenses with resultant greater resistance to awareness. For example, if the child uses denial, he now may manifest more denial; if he is "acting out," there may be an even greater flurry of such "acting out" behavior that is antithetical to development of greater awareness. An illustration of a therapist's error in this regard and of the patient's negative response is seen in the following clinical example.

> Jeff was a nine-year-old boy who repeatedly tried to pull at his therapist's tie during a session to which he had come acting very silly and infantile. The therapist did not bother to establish with Jeff how his regressed infantile stance at the moment appeared to be a powerful defense against the affect of anger. Rather he summarily interpreted to Jeff, "What you would like to do is pull at my penis." Jeff responded with an increased tempo in his regressed behavior. He now tried even more diligently to get at his therapist's tie while he chanted mockingly, "I want my doctor's tie and his penis." He then ended up taking several jabs at his therapist's genitals.

As with any content in psychotherapy, it is important that the therapist use the patient's manifest behavior or productions as a bridge to get at hidden conflicts and impulses. For example, "Even as you talk of how very much afraid you were as you watched the horror movie on TV, you sound excited as though there was also some fun in it for you," can serve as a prelude to consideration of the patient's sadomasochistic impulses. A similar situation prevailed in the treatment of an obsessional boy who vehemently fought his preoccupation with homosexual thoughts. His therapist observed, "A person ordinarily ends up working overtime at fighting something for which he feels some fascination." Thereby he assisted his patient to consider his homosexual impulses and conflicts over these impulses.

It is important for the therapist to remember to use the manifest content as a bridge to the latent but not to negate the legitimacy or even deny the existence of the manifest in favor of the latent content. It must be most disconcerting for patients to hear the ill-advised but so often heard comment from therapists, "But what you really think . . . ," or "But what you really mean . . . ," or "But how you really feel. . . ." In this manner the therapist virtually ignores the child's expressed content in his haste to launch into exploration of "hidden treasures." In another sense it is as though the therapist were cynical enough to believe that the only reality is the hidden reality.

While the therapist may be very unrealistic if he cannot look for hidden meanings or unconscious factors in his patient's productions, for him to be in search of innuendo and to virtually ignore the manifest does entail its own unreality. It would appear to be more sound as well as more understandable to even the more heavily defended child if the therapist would openly weigh and balance the various facets of the material at hand. For example, he might observe, "Even while you say that you detest what your brother does to you, it strikes me that you also have some other feelings about his behavior toward you." From here he can then refer to the cues in the patient's previous behavior or verbal productions that lead him to conclude that there are other feelings, with which he now specifically confronts the child.

The second general category of content includes the elements of the child's relationship with his therapist. Specifically herein are included the various transference manifestations to which the therapist needs to be attuned as he looks to the child's outside therapy contacts and his earlier experiences so as to account for the child's particular reactions to him that are not relevant to what transpires between them at the moment. The amount of attention the therapist elects to pay to this facet of therapy or whether he even chooses to deal with it directly in therapy will need to be determined by the nature of this particular therapy and upon the goals that have been established. Accordingly, the more reliance there is on the therapeutic effectiveness of the relationship itself, the more the therapist will rely on the development and the maintenance of positive transference reactions. Therefore, he will more quickly deal with negative transference reactions so as to obliterate them. The more the therapy leans toward the "uncovering" variety in which emphasis is placed on the development of a more general awareness about self and about interactions with others, the more will the therapist wish transference reactions to unfold more fully with their variegated patterns of positive and negative elements. Therefore, the therapist in this instance will proceed more slowly in the handling of transference reactions, as he realizes that a relative transference neurosis will never have an opportunity to unfold if the child's transference distortions are corrected virtually as they manifest themselves.

REASON FOR INTERVENTION

When does the therapist intervene? Why does he intervene at a particular time? The prime danger is that the therapist may intervene because he feels he needs to do something. Or he may intervene impertinently because he has a "hot" bit of insight which he feels compelled to share with his child patient. While it is difficult to be very specific as to when a therapist should intervene, there are some guidelines according to which the therapist can decide whether or not to do so.

First, he may need to intervene so as to create a therapeutic structure. Such would be the case especially early in a child's therapy when the therapist in effect may still be introducing the child to the whole process of therapy which may be such a totally novel experience for him. We are reminded of Anna Freud's (1946) earlier recommendation in child analysis for an "introductory phase" which she felt had nothing to do with the real analytical work. She in effect saw this to be the period in which she was "inducing an insight into the trouble, imparting confidence in the analyst, and turning the decision for analysis from one taken by others into his own." Or, "it is simply a matter of converting an unsuitable situation into a desirable one, by all the means which are at the disposal of an adult dealing with a child."

Though such a formal introductory phase ordinarily is no longer considered necessary for child analysis or child therapy, there still is a need for the therapist to introduce his child patient early in therapy to the whole idea of therapy so as to encourage him to commit himself to a therapeutic alliance with his psychotherapist. Such introduction not only ought to be made to the child in his early contacts with his therapist during assessment and during formal discussions about the contemplated therapy but even as he begins his therapy visits; however, early interventions ought still be directed toward the creation of a therapeutic structure. For example, early in therapy it may be a matter of repeatedly calling the child's attention to the fact that he regularly refers to therapy as "school" either by slips of the tongue or by practically raising his hand to be called upon and be given permission before he ventures to say anything or engage in any activity.

Whereas the therapist initially intervenes as above so as to create the desired therapeutic structure, later in the course of therapy he repeatedly may need to intervene similarly in order to maintain this structure. For example, he may repeatedly need to deal with the child's continued need to ask permission to eat candy, chew gum, or to leave the room to go to the lavatory, though the therapist has regularly attempted to convey to the child that as therapist he does not assume the role of the usual adult figure in the child's life, i.e. he is not the authority figure who tells the child what he is to do or is not to do and upon whom the child depends for permission to act or not act. In such a therapeutic structure the therapist would need to emphasize his aim to examine behavior for purposes of understanding more fully its nature and its determinants.

Another reason to intervene is to enhance the therapeutic process. In effect, the task at hand is to maintain some sort of reasonable equilibrium between regression and progression that will allow for a productive therapeutic process. Accordingly, interventions can be directed in several different directions. First, there are interventions to enhance regression. Such interventions usually will consist primarily of much reassurance from the therapist that he is accepting of the child in his behavior. For example, the child may need continual reassurance that it is okay for him to be spontaneously active and to talk about feelings which he fears will initiate angry retorts or criticism from his therapist. In effect, the therapist so intervenes as to encourage spontaneity and generally more freedom from the inhibited, constricted child. From another standpoint it may be that the therapist needs to make efforts to help the child become free through modification of his excessively severe superego restrictions.

There are other times when the therapist may need to intervene so as to curb regression when such behavior leaves the child stalemated, as he now virtually regresses for the sake of regression and no therapeutic advantage is to be derived. Interventions run the spectrum of interventions. There are those aimed toward helping him be aware of his behavior and its various determinants so as to enhance his conscious, volitional mastery. In other instances the therapist may need to set limits. Lastly, physical restriction or restraint may be in order when the patient becomes destructive or assaultive in his regression. A clinical illustration of how interpretive comments might be used to stem regressive behavior is seen in the following clinical example.

Sue, an eight-year-old neurotic girl, danced into the office for her therapy session in a silly, provocative manner right after her therapist had talked privately with her mother. Sue proceeded to bounce in her chair as she began to chant a number of things about her mother. She was all over her chair, acting especially silly as she finally began to chant, "Daddy pees in mama's hair." The therapist at this point observed for Sue that her silliness followed upon his private session with her mother. He related her silly behavior to her apparent concern about what she imagined had transpired between her mother and him even as she apparently must be concerned about what she imagined to happen when her mother and father were alone together at home. Her hyperactivity with all its regressive features ceased abruptly as Sue now sat in her chair looking sad and pensive.

Also in this series of interventions are those geared to enhancement of progression. As such, the therapist not only aims to stem regression but he actively encourages progression. For example, emphasis might be placed on reinforcing the fact that the "big boy" (or "big girl") way to cope with problems is to talk about them and to try to work out solutions in that manner. Implicit in this comment, and perhaps explicitly stated somewhere along the way, would be the idea that for him to constantly lose his temper and to carry on a scene or to engage in any of a number of other regressive maneuvers whenever he is crossed or frustrated just does not lend itself to resolution of the problems of growing up.

Another group of interventions are those by which the therapist lends support to a child through assistance with particular personality functioning. So it may be that the therapist needs to give him an "ego boost" or moral support as the child struggles with some particular difficulty, or the therapist may more regularly need to offer him assistance in an area of ego or superego functioning in which he evidences deficiency. The child with deficiency in reality testing, for example, may regularly require assistance from his therapist in the assessment of reality even while he is afforded an opportunity to examine how his own denial and projection interfere with his ability to appraise himself and his world in any sort of realistic fashion. Or the child who lacks impulse control may need various types of assistance from his therapist. These will range from anticipation of the emergence of what is likely to set him off to curtailment of activity and even physical restraint when the child gets beyond his own controls.

Similar considerations are in order when confronted with the child who evidences deficiencies in superego functioning in which the child is lacking. Accordingly, it may be that the therapist needs to confront the child with his behavior so as to help him convert ego syntonic behavior into ego dystonic behavior, i.e. to help him feel uncomfortable or uneasy about behavior to which he is currently indifferent or in which he even enjoys engaging but in either event his reaction is to his own detriment. To accomplish this end, the therapist does not reprimand the child for his behavior but confronts him with a realistic assessment of his behavior—a value judgment on the basis of developmental expectations but not a moral judgment. For example, when faced with the pubertal child who in his anger regularly pouts and sulks rather than talks about what distresses him, the therapist might let him know, "You are acting like a two-year-old," without either directly or by innuendo conveying the message that he therefore is a "bad boy."

Or it may be a matter of in effect helping the child "pat himself on the back" when because of his severely punitive superego he feels that he just cannot do anything deserving of praise. The aim here would be to help him establish his own inner "voice of conscience" from which he might derive a sense of satisfaction for his "good" behavior. So the emphasis is not on "I'm glad you are behaving so or not doing such and such," but on "It must make you feel good to have done so well" or "It is understandable that you would feel proud of accomplishing what you did." Encouragement of the child to use the therapist as a model for identification in reference to behavior—as undoubtedly the therapist is, whether or not he chooses to become one—centers around approbation of the child's self-appraisal. That is, the therapist's emphasis remains on, "I am approving of your frank, realistic appraisal of yourself and I am approving of the good feelings you experience for a job well done in that regard."

MODE OF INTERVENTION

How does the therapist make an intervention in therapy? This question may elicit a response like "By talking with him, of course! How else?" In reading the answer, it may seem enigmatic, for one can imagine it to be much broader than what is conveyed explicitly by the words, i.e. the answer might be a simple exclamation of surprise or it might be a disguised way of responding sarcastically to what was taken to be a provocative question. While it is true that much of intervening in psychotherapy does and ought to entail verbalization, the nonverbal accompaniments always need to be considered, as illustrated in the above answer to a question. In fact, even as the essence of a message, so the essence of an intervention may be in nonverbal communication. But a word of caution is in order. If the therapist should rely on a nonverbal intervention, it is generally wise that he in effect explain his behavior to the patient especially if there is any chance at all of a misinterpretation of his action, as behavior may so easily lend itself to a variety of interpretations because of what lies in the eye of the beholder. Such considerations will especially need to be kept in mind if the patient has problems centering around nonverbal communications. For example, the patient may have characterological problems so that he lives in a whirlwind of repeated nonverbal communications to which he remains oblivious as they escape his awareness. Verbalizations to him may be especially important.

The point in any event is that the therapist needs to be aware of his nonverbal communications as much as possible. As a corollary, he needs to avoid use of nonverbal communication which left by itself is vague and lends itself to a variety of interpretations. For example, though a shrug of the shoulders may actually be very effective and convey more than one could with a million words, its poignancy might be sharpened with an added unequivocal "What can I say?" in response to the provocateur or in response to the obsessive rationalizer. The greatest danger in letting a non-verbal intervention stand by itself lies in the fact that the patient may construe it to be a chastisement when it was not so meant. Furthermore, exclusive reliance on the non-verbal may add up to the therapist's way of expressing countertransference reactions which he finds so difficult to handle.

The simplest forms of nonverbal interventions might be signals of pleasure, such as a smile, or of displeasure, such as a frown. The most complex form of nonverbal interventions, even while the grossest form, is physical contact, either to restrain the aggressive and/or destructive child or to show affection to the emotionally needy child patient. Indiscriminate reliance on either needs to be questioned. There are times when physical restraint is in order so as to maintain some physical integrity of body and setting. Furthermore, with some severely disturbed children, especially those who persistently maintain feelings of omnipotence, there are times when nothing short of physical restraint will make them accessible to other therapeutic interventions geared toward aiding them control themselves in a reasonable fashion. The task for the therapist is not to try to prove to the child that he is more omnipotent than the child—and there is danger the therapist might intervene from this position—rather he needs to try to take the business of the moment out of the arena, out of a power struggle, and proceed from the position of trying to maintain or create a reasonable therapeutic structure that follows the rules of civilization wherein relatively unlimited verbal expression is encouraged but limits need to be placed on motoric expression. Or the therapist might let the child know that in therapy he stands by a very literal interpretation of the age-old childhood adage, "Sticks and stones will break my bones but names will never hurt me." An illustration of how physical restraint was necessary in therapy and of how the child responded in a positive manner to such an intervention is seen in the following clinical vignette.

Sandra was a nine-year-old girl who was placed in residential treatment after she had presented with severe behavior problems at home and in school. In therapy Sandra picked up where she had left off at home. Provocative vulgarity led to open attacks on anything and everything in the therapist's office, including the therapist, even as Sandra appeared more and more fearful of any sort of positive relationship with her male therapist. Confrontations and interpretations of her behavior over the span of several weeks rang hollow. Finally, the therapist sat Sandra in a chair and held her there while he told her that he would hold her there until she was able to control herself. It turned out that he found it necessary to hold her there most of the session.

The following day when the therapist was on her ward in the hospital, Sandra stopped momentarily to say coyly, "I love you," and then ran off down the hall. While there was no doubt that her statement was open to a variety of interpretations, there also was no doubt that there was a sincere ring to what she said. Furthermore, there was a marked change in her behavior in subsequent sessions, as she now engaged in play and became more able to talk with her therapist.

In such use of physical restraint it is essential that the therapist explicitly verbalize his intentions and openly assess reality for the patient so as to keep the transference and countertransference distortions to a minimum. Accordingly, the therapist in the above noted clinical interchange told Sandra explicitly that he would hold her until she evidenced some ability to control herself. Her protests to the contrary, he let her know he was not out to hurt her but was holding her so she could not hurt him or destroy his possessions. In response to her protests that he was hurting her, the therapist kept reminding her that being held firmly was bound to be painful if she fought so desperately to free herself.

There are several factors to keep in mind in the consideration of such intervention of physical restraint. The relative size and age of the child are important. The therapist instinctively may realize that he stands nothing to gain if he himself ends up in a headlock applied to him by his patient. He also ought to recognize that physical restraint might generally be more effective and less complicated in the younger child, and it is the younger, still more motorically inclined child who is more likely to demand such intervention. At any age the possibility of sexual stimulation needs to be kept in mind, as the physical restraint can become a veritable masochistic experience for the child. Because of all these factors plus the fact that such physical restraint militates against the relative detachment of the therapist if he tries to minimize the "real person" in attempts to be more of the transference figure, some maintain that the therapist should never physically restrain his patient. Some, for example, will merely terminate a session if the child comes to the point of demanding physical restraint. While termination of a session is worthwhile and effective in therapy of the child who has some commitment to therapy as reflected in at least the beginning of a therapeutic alliance, with others the termination of sessions accomplishes nothing, as the child gains what he originally wanted and in the process he maintains fantasies of omnipotence that he again in fact proves to be realistic.

To discuss physical restraint at some length ought not to be construed as advocating its use but rather as an indication that physical restraint in therapy is not to be taken lightly, be the therapist for or against its use. The following is offered as a reasonable stand on the subject. While the therapist is accepting of the fact that if worse comes to worse, physical restraint may be specifically indicated, premature consideration of this option ought not nip in the bud consideration of more innovative ways of mobilizing the child's own inner controls. To include physical restraint as a legitimate option, however, may help the therapist not need to fall back on unrealistic cajolement and bribery to maintain some semblance of a therapeutic structure.

The therapist's physical contacts of an affectionate nature

also ought not to be taken lightly. There obviously are a number of different ways that different therapists are inclined to approach children. Some quite naturally are inclined to put a hand on a child's shoulder or tussle a child's hair. Weighted against this inclination must be consideration of the manner in which the child perceives such physical overtures and the sort of tone they set for the relationship. Used extensively, such physical overtures smack of the overseer "being nice" to his underling, i.e. they certainly can emphasize an inequality between the therapist and the child and set the stage for a paternalistic approach by the therapist. There are times, however, when nothing short of some affectionate or comforting physical overtures will suffice for the child. The extremely frightened youngster literally may be in desperate need of a comforting hand. Or with the extremely disturbed child who is especially dificient in his ability to develop a relationship, to hold him on the lap and to stroke him may be essential for the development of a relationship, as he approaches the therapist essentially as an infant who will build a relationship on the bedrock of repeated bodily contacts.

Another consideration in a discussion of the manner in which to intervene is the matter of whether the therapist chooses to get at the intrapsychic substrata of the child's productions by a direct or indirect route, i.e. the therapist first of all can get at these intrapsychic elements by proceeding there directly from the child's productions. Accordingly, he proceeds in the usual fashion of going from defense to impulse as he aims to help the patient expand his horizons and depths of awareness. The therapist in this way directly confronts the child with his productions as derivatives of his intrapsychic functioning.

There is a second way in which the therapist can get at the intrapsychic elements with the child patient. He can deal with these elements indirectly through the medium of play. Though there is a full discussion of play in the chapter devoted to play therapy, some comments about play therapy are germane to the discussion at hand. In effect, rather than proceed directly from the child's productions to his intrapsychic functioning, the therapist relies on getting his message across to the child through the play even as the child communicates to him via the play, i.e. therapy proceeds in displacement. The therapist may ask questions of the puppets or dolls and they will be the ones to respond. In this manner it appears as though the child conveys their messages rather than the fact that they convey his messages. In effect the child and his therapist proceed to play "make-believe" even while they implicitly acknowledge that they both know about whom and about what they are talking. To engage in therapy in the displacement of play does offer a child the opportunity to maintain a comfortable distance between himself and his frightening inner struggles, and this distance may allow for a greater freedom to observe himself. With some children who readily engage in play, most or even all of therapy can be carried on in this fashion so that there may never be a need to bring the material out of displacement.

In the usual therapy of children it is not a simple "either/ or" matter as to whether the therapist proceeds directly to intrapsychic matters or whether he deals with them in the displacement of play. Among the various vicissitudes of therapy itself, the child's relative ability to discriminate between play and reality will ordinarily be a major determinant of the course to follow. First, chances are that the child who finds it difficult to discriminate between play and reality may also find it difficult to engage in play therapy in a fashion that lends itself to handling his productions in displacement. Second, the therapist may with justification discourage or at least not encourage the child to involve himself in play if he recognizes that such matters are hardly "make-believe" for the child either because of the child's complete identification with characters in play or because of his relatively complete dissociation from the characters he portrays.

In either instance, be it the child who balks at play or

be it the therapist who decides that play is not in order at the moment, the therapist may need to pave the way for meaningful play by first of all dealing directly with the child's emotional functioning. Accordingly, it may be a matter of dealing with the reasons why the child cannot engage in play. The process entails an exploration of the child's fears to the extent that they are neurotic and the cementing of a more secure relationship with the therapist to the extent that the child evidences marked deficiencies in various ego functions. Or if it is the therapist who feels a need to put the brakes on the child's play, he may first need to help the child see how he uses massive projection, displacement, and/or regression in play to get away from painful realities before the child's involvement in play can become more therapeutically meaningful.

OUTSIDE INTERVENTIONS

There are also a host of interventions that a therapist may elect to make in the child's life outside the therapy sessions. To talk about such contacts outside therapy sessions gets us into the whole area of "environmental manipulation" that some may consider alien to or even opposed to psychotherapy. In another sense there is the risk of talking about another "kettle of fish." Nonetheless, there is merit in consideration of the interventions placed outside therapy sessions in discussion of psychotherapeutic strategy, as these may be essential to maintain the psychotherapy of the child or at least may have their impact on the child's therapy by virtue of how they color the child's relationship with his therapist. The most common of these interventions are those made in the child's home through contacts with his family. Such interventions are discussed fully in the chapter on family considerations. From the standpoint of the child's own psychotherapy, such interventions are intended primarily to help establish an adequate therapeutic structure and to enhance psychotherapy. Similar considerations are applicable regarding interventions in the community at large, be it school or court. For example, the therapist may decide it is essential to have the school provide more of a structure or a particular type of structure for the child so as to enhance therapy. Or he may advocate a particular type of court involvement with the child and his family, as he deems it essential to effective psychotherapy.

Just as the therapist who aims for a reasonable approach to therapy does not intervene with the child in therapy sessions simply for the sake of intervening, so he ought to proceed in a similar manner with outside interventions. Some are inclined to advocate a very active involvement of the child's therapist in the child's life outside of the therapy sessions, as they stress a need for him to have frequent contacts with the child's family and school. While such may be the case with some children, especially those who manifest behavior problems that keep everybody in a chronic state of agitation, in the therapy of many children the therapist will find little or no need for outside contacts except for an occasional contact with the child's parents.

Even when the therapist feels there is need for him to have contact with the child's family or school, he has to keep in mind the limitations inherent in such contacts. What he has to contribute may be minimal, and the impact of his contribution may be minimized even further by virtue of the fact that the message he has to offer may be difficult both to transmit and to receive. Most usually it will be his task to help the parents and others involved with the child to understand the child and his problems more fully or in such a light that they are better able to interact more effectively with him. There is danger that those involved with the child may look to the therapist for ready answers, but what they receive may leave them frustrated, for they are looking to him for solutions while he concentrates on attempts at understanding that will assist them to arrive at their own solutions. The therapist's usefulness in such contacts might best be viewed in terms of the assistance that he can provide in conjunction with therapy in the arrangement of a structure that is conducive to the child's general development. The therapist may be hard pressed to outline an ideal structure to be tailored for a particular child, and in fact there is something utopian about thinking in terms of ideal structures. The more reasonable goal for him is to try to work toward a structure in which all participants, the child and all those with whom he comes in contact, might communicate more openly with one another so that in this manner they may be more able to work things out for themselves.

It also needs to be remembered that the therapist can become very unrealistic in his expectations of family and school. Even as he has all his attention focused on this child in therapy, he may verily act as though everyone in the child's total environment needs to center his attention around this child. In the process of concentrating on what he concludes that his child patient needs, he may lose sight of the bigger picture. As a result, his recommendations may be totally unrealistic. Accordingly, it may be folly to expect a teacher to give this particular child virtually one-to-one attention when she also has twenty-five to thirty other children in her classroom.

SPECIAL CONSIDERATIONS

There are a number of considerations about children and child psychotherapy that a therapist needs to keep in mind as he engages with his child patient in therapy. Uppermost among these considerations is the fact that the child may be especially sensitive to the stock question of the stereotyped therapist, "why?" in reference to thoughts, feelings, or actions. Much to his consternation the child may have learned that such a question from an adult usually amounts to a rhetorical question used to convey a reprimand when the adult is feeling especially frustrated and helpless. Because of the child's sensitivity in this regard some therapists have recommended that the therapist make statements to elicit responses rather than ask questions. One therapist reported that after she adopted this practice one of her patients made a comment to express her fascination with the fact that the therapist "told" her questions.

The issue is not whether the therapist concentrates on "telling" questions or asking them. Rather the child needs to learn that the therapist's "why's" are not a euphemistic way of telling him to "shape up." There is the danger that in therapy to ask "why" may become just that rather than a genuine invitation to investigate the content at hand. For example, the therapist may become especially assiduous in his pursuit of the "why" for aggressive behavior, as he is actually trying to curb it in this devious manner, while he is not nearly as diligent in the pursuit of the "why" for reaction formation, as he has no trouble in dealing with the passive, conforming child. In this way, the therapist may confirm what the child already believed: "He's only interested in my behaving. He doesn't want to understand what I am doing, but he merely wants me to be a good boy." Perhaps at any given point when the child's behavior in therapy is becoming a problem, it might be more reasonable for the therapist to very openly let the child know that his behavior is unacceptable for whatever the reasons might be and then proceed to exploration of its determinants. It would seem preferable for a therapist to act in such an openly direct manner than for him to cajole the child into changing his behavior by a ruse of asking him "why."

It also needs to be kept in mind that what for an adult would constitute a confrontation, as he is conscious of the particular content, for a child would virtually entail an interpretation, as the content escapes his awareness. Such, for example, is the case with affect. The child just may not be aware of how he feels, and he may not be inclined to think in terms of feelings as he thinks primarily in terms of action. Opposed to such a state is one in which the child merely lacks a clear definition of various affects. In the latter instance the therapist will need to deal with ignorance rather than with repression; he will need to inform rather than interpret.

Akin to what is alluded to above, psychotherapy of the child involves considerable education. This feature was discussed in part earlier in this chapter, but several things were left unsaid. There are a number of areas in which this education is especially centered. As was emphasized earlier, education in therapy is and ought to be centered around education about therapy itself. There are several areas in which such education is especially appropriate. First, Anna Freud's (1946) introductory phase essentially involved an education concerning what therapy is about. In current practice the early phase of therapy to varying degrees according to the needs of a particular child needs to entail education concerning the process of therapy itself. Second, there is the education involved in matters like labeling feelings for the child. In effect, the therapist herein educates the child as to how people are inclined to view themselves and to communicate their inner states. As noted previously, such orientation of the child by the therapist will be especially important to the extent that the child is inclined to think in terms of action or readily manifest behavior rather than in terms of feelings.

Third, there is the education involved in setting limits, which so many times does become part of child therapy as noted earlier in this chapter. Fourth, there may be a need for education in therapy in certain life experiences in which the child has been lacking either because of his age or because of his own particular circumstances. For example, the therapist may need to educate a child about games. While the child's parents may have taught him that "it's only a game," to help him repress his untoward reactions to a loss, the therapist may need to take a moment to help the child assess the whole game situation more realistically; for example, "It may be only a game but it's also true that it's ordinarily more fun winning than losing. Furthermore, it's understandable that a guy might feel mad about losing, though blowing one's stack when feeling mad over a game is another matter." Without such education, which admittedly does also include some attempts to attenuate the superego prohibition "Thou shalt not get mad," games may not lend themselves to therapeutic use, as personal reactions are not allowed to emerge.

In these and all other educative attempts in which a therapist decides to engage, he still needs to avoid becoming nothing more than another educator of the child. He can easily slip into the position of answering apparently benign questions about any of a number of subjects about which adults are supposedly more learned than are children—so the child may insist. Such an approach by the child may be part of powerful resistance to therapy in several ways. For example, in this manner he may latch onto benign subjects or he may maintain a controlled dependence on one who may appear so awesome to him.

There are also several developmental and psychopathological considerations that the therapist needs to keep in mind as he engages in therapy with the child. One very specific consideration is the difficulty borderline children have in utilization of interpretations, as noted by Anna Freud (1965). She observes that with an interpretation to the borderline child, "the usual relief and ego control of the fantasy world do not follow. Instead the very wording of the analytic interpretation is taken up by the patient and woven into a continued and increased flow of anxiety-arousing fantasy." Such inability to utilize an interpretation is seen in the therapy of Mary, a twelve-year-old borderline psychotic girl.

> Mary started her therapy session by demanding that her therapist do various things in the office. After some initial compliance with Mary's demands, the therapist noted to Mary her obvious need to be very controlling. Rather than pause in her activity, Mary not only continued her demands at an ever-increasing tempo but she unobtrusively added a theme about people controlling people to her steady stream of chatter.

Among the more general considerations is the therapist's need to consider the gradations of his being a "real" person (in contrast to a transference object) according to the child's needs on the basis of development and psychopathology. Specifically, he will need to be more of a "real" person with the younger child (especially the preschool child) and with the child with greater ego and superego deficiencies, regardless of age. In effect, the more the therapist becomes an educator, the more he becomes a "real" person to the patient.

There are several types of ego and superego deficiencies that especially demand that the therapist take the stance of a "real" person. Such is the case when he is engaged with the child who evidences a severe disturbance in object relationships. In this case it may be his task to help the child establish an object relationship or to nurture some growth in this regard while he attempts to help remove whatever psychological roadblocks to such development do exist. For example, the therapist needs to become very much of a "real" person when he deals with the autistic child who evidences practically naught when it comes to interacting with others. To a different degree he may need to be a "real" person with the child who is essentially symbiotic or at least markedly dependent in his manner of relating. In this latter instance the child's inability to function with any semblance of independence may necessitate that the therapist allow for perpetuation of such manner of relating so as to encourage some sort of therapeutic relationship from which further growth might spring.

The degree of the child's reality testing and development of his inner controls will also determine the extent to which a therapist needs to become a "real" person in therapy. Again the issue revolves around how much of an educator the therapist will need to become because of the child's lack of experiential exposure on the basis of age, personal pathological interferences, or the nature of his environment.

Similar considerations about the nature of the relationship toward which to strive need to be weighed when it comes to the child's superego functioning. For example, a child with a so-called "corruptible" superego or one with a stringent superego might demand some bending by the therapist away from being the more strictly a "transference figure" so as to become more of a model of identification by which to help the child tighten up the laxity or attenuate the severity of his superego functioning.

Another situation prevails with the child who presents with "superego lacunae" so that in effect he does not experience guilt in response to given bits of deviant behavior. The task will be to generate anxiety about behavior that will lead to internalized prohibitions where such are sorely lacking.

Another important consideration in psychotherapy of the child is the need for the therapist to realize that any intervention he makes in therapy sessions is likely to be effective only to the extent that he and the patient have established a "therapeutic alliance" or "working alliance." To establish such an alliance with a child may be a difficult task especially to the extent that it was not his idea to come in the first place and to the extent that he feels no need to be party to a venture he sees as geared to change him. At best he then may feel that even as it was his adult parent who brought him to therapy, so it is now the adult therapist who is to resolve his problems. As such he may not see the need for his active involvement in therapy that is actually so vital to meaningful psychotherapeutic work. Combined with this is the personal investment in his particular behavior that a child is bound to have, be it symptomatic to others or troublesome to him. The fact is that the behavior is also adaptive, and as such he can be expected to be reluctant to part with it. To be forced to give up a part of himself may be exactly how he views therapy, as he sees the therapist as someone trying to take something from him. The end result is that therapy may become too much of a tussle, as far as the patient is concerned. Accordingly, the therapist's interventions are viewed as parries and thrusts to which he is to respond accordingly. It is because of an unestablished working alliance that interventions may so often seem to fall on deaf ears in child therapy. Rather than appreciate the problem to be one of a nonexistent working alliance, the therapist may be too quick to conclude, for example, that children for the most part are not receptive and responsive to interpretive comments about their behavior. What he may neglect to see in the process is the fact that the child does not see himself involved in a "therapeutic alliance" but that he sees himself engaged in a "therapeutic battle" in which he needs to defend himself and needs to resist the therapist.

A vital consideration that needs to be taken into account in the preparation and the subsequent implementation of the strategy of psychotherapy is the matter of how therapy works. For example, if, as was mentioned earlier in this chapter, the therapist intervenes in order to initiate or perpetuate the process of therapy, he needs to have in mind some idea of what the whole process of therapy entails. Within this understanding he then needs to appreciate what he hopes to accomplish with a particular patient, since what he sees to be therapeutic for his patient ought to determine how, when, and even by what means he intervenes in therapy. In an earlier chapter the various factors that account for therapeutic effectiveness were discussed within the framework of trying to arrive at a conceptual model for child psychotherapy. It would seem appropriate at this time to consider these factors with concentration on specifically how each factor might be taken into account by the therapist as he proceeds in his psychotherapeutic work.

First, there are the benefits in psychotherapy that accrue from the relationship itself. These include the support of personality functioning the child receives as he "leans" on the therapist. Stress on this as the healing principle might be reflected in an encouragement of the process of identification with his therapist. With this in mind the therapist might especially strive to help the child maintain a positive relationship with him.

Second, there is the "corrective emotional experience" derived from therapy. The therapist might follow this principle according to Alexander's conceptualization of "corrective emotional experience" as essentially a process in which the therapist structures therapy so that his approach or reaction to the patient counteracts the child's earlier deleterious experiences. For example, approval may be emphasized where previously the child experienced unrealistically extensive disapproval, or "giving" to the child is accentuated so as to counteract earlier experience of deprivation. The therapist might also view this principle as applicable to all of the experiences that the child is bound to enjoy in his spontaneous interactions in therapy. Accordingly, he may then see therapy to involve a corrective emotional experience in the sense that it offers the child an opportunity to see himself in a more realistic manner, to express himself in a more reasonable fashion, and to interact with an adult in a more meaningful way. The therapist might see this principle of therapy to be especially crucial for the child patient whose opportunities for wider experience are limited and who is more bound to the paradigm of interaction derived from the particular relationship(s) he enjoys with his parent(s). In any event, here as with the other factors considered to account for therapeutic effectiveness, the therapist might emphasize this factor as *the* essential healing principle or he might look on it as a by-product of any therapy that proceeds reasonably well.

Third, there is the role of catharsis or abreaction as a possible principle of therapeutic effectiveness. Though Anna Freud (1965) notes that child therapists were later to recognize that catharsis alone was not sufficient, there is no denying that catharsis can and does play a part in successful therapy of children. This principle might be emphasized in itself or within the overall therapeutic process and strategy planned accordingly. The degree to which it is emphasized may well be determined by the extent to which the therapist views the child as experiencing repeated crises that lend themselves to pent-up emotion or to traumatic experiences that generate affect with which the child may then begin to deal in various maladaptive ways that are reflected in developmental distortions. While attempts at abreaction or catharsis might be emphasized in reference to a specific traumatic event, more often than not it would appear that catharsis or abreaction might be seen as but the step, and a vital one at that, which generates affect with which the child is then helped to cope in a manner other than by utilization of repressive forces.

Fourth, persuasion or suggestion may also add its part to the overall effectiveness of therapy. While there is room for disagreement with Frank's contention that the effectiveness of psychotherapy rests primarily on suggestion, there is no denying that it must be a powerful force in all of psychotherapy. As with the other principles listed, the therapist may rely on it implicitly or he may explicitly call upon it. To rely on persuasion implicitly is to proceed with the realization that this principle is operative already to the extent that the child and his family come, agreeably or reluctantly, with the idea that such visits are geared toward improvement in personal functioning, be the malfunction what it might. The effectiveness of this implicit suggestion is enhanced further to the extent that the child and/or his parents agree with the therapist on desired improvement and to the extent that all share a relatively "common assumptive world," i.e. a similar sense of values in reference to overall personal functioning.

To talk of a therapist explicitly calling on persuasion or suggestion may conjure up images of hypnosis. While hypnosis as such must be rare in child therapy, practices based on suggestion would seem to be fairly widespread. For example, when the therapist emphasizes the importance of the relationship in his therapeutic strategy, he not only falls back implicitly on suggestion in the sense noted above, but chances are that he more explicitly will rely on the effectiveness of this principle. Advisory comments to the child and/or parents will most likely be viewed as coming from the one in authority, whether or not the therapist wishes to view his role in that light, and most likely will end up weighted with the power of suggestion. On the basis of Glover's comment that any incomplete interpretation is a suggestion, when the therapist shares insights or makes interpretive comments he may be actively utilizing suggestions more than he is inclined to recognize.

Fifth, there is therapeutic effectiveness through the development of greater awareness or insight. Again, this principle as with the other principles noted above may be viewed as likely to operate in successful therapy and, as such, likely to enhance therapeutic effectiveness, or it might be viewed as a prime healing force so that efforts are planned to actively employ its operation. In the former case, one or more of the other principles may be emphasized. In the latter case the other principles are most likely seen as important to the extent that they set the stage for the development of ever greater awareness. To emphasize the effectiveness of this principle is to emphasize in therapy confrontations and interpretations within the context of transference development. The aim is in effect to help the child become ever more aware of situations or interactions in which he is involved.

Sixth and last, there is the need to consider among the various principles that account for therapeutic effectiveness the impact of so-called "maturational pull" that perhaps enhances the effectiveness of whatever is done in therapy even while it itself is enhanced by whatever is done in therapy. "Maturational pull" might be conceptualized as an inner directive force, derived both from innate, constitutional factors and from internalized environmental expectations. It is this force that inclines the child of himself toward more mature development that is manifested essentially in more independent functioning. In another sense, we are not talking about a therapeutic that the therapist applies directly but rather about the guiding principle around which all therapeutic principles are applied. With this in mind the therapist structures therapy and makes his moves in a manner that leads to removal of the roadblocks that interfere with the normal process of maturation.

TERMINATION

Once therapy has been instituted, when to terminate such therapy does become a prime consideration even though at the moment it may be held in abeyance. On the other hand it might also be said that a discussion of termination needs to include consideration of the initiation of therapy. The two go hand in hand, at least to the extent that it might be said that termination is in order when one has accomplished the task he set for himself at the beginning of therapy. Many times the goal which is set is vague enough when the therapist talks with the child in terms of helping him develop greater self-awareness or insight. To set such general goals ordinarily allows for proceeding indefinitely in therapy and from that standpoint is desirable to the extent that attempts are geared to "uncovering" psychotherapy. Yet there are advantages in so much of child psychotherapy in proceeding in a two-stage fashion, somewhat as follows.

In this context the first stage of therapy involves attempts at resolution of the particular problem with which the patient presents. Upon resolution of this problem in weeks or several months, as is the case with a number of children who come to a psychotherapist, there can then be a reconsideration of the total situation with an eye to whether or not to proceed any further. Admittedly there are a number of patients with whom such an approach is not appropriate, as their problems are of a long-standing nature with well-established neurotic patterns operative so that intensive psychotherapy over an extended period of time seems indicated at the very beginning. However, there are so many times that a child reaches a therapist with a recently erupted symptom, be it school refusal, a phobia, an obsessive compulsive phenomenon, or a behavioral outburst of one variety or another. Either because of their own anxiety or because of community pressure, the parents in the heat of the moment may commit themselves to more than is realistic for them, as they feel compelled to do something and to do it quickly. As they feel helpless and feel there are no alternatives, they may be willing to commit themselves to anything. They may have second thoughts later when things settle down a bit.

Chances are that the therapist, too, may find things to be different in a moment of less heat when the need to do something seems less urgent. Though the initial assessment of the child's overall development will give indications for the greater or lesser need for circumscribed problem-oriented therapy or therapy geared toward alteration of neurotic problems and as such probably long-term therapy, the picture regarding desirability of therapy may change after things settle down a bit. The therapist may find altered motivations, for example, that may make his original recommendations less reasonable if it is a long-term commitment that was demanded.

The converse may also be true as the therapist finds "more than he bargained for" once he has the child and family involved in therapy and more work seems indicated than originally anticipated. Yet as a group, therapists seem more inclined to see pathology in a particular type of adaptation and are less likely to see the positive elements in a particular type of functioning, so that a tendency to overdiagnose ordinarily is a more prevalent vulnerability than is the tendency to underdiagnose.

To be flexible regarding termination entails essentially a matter of paying attention to some very useful guidelines that are ordinarily provided very naturally during the course of therapy. It involves paying close attention to the process of therapy so as to be aware of points along the way that lend themselves well to termination.

The first point that lends itself to termination is at the time of symptomatic improvement. The child, for example, has presented with symptoms of a school refusal, physical symptoms that reflect emotional turmoil or a phobia. After several weeks or even months the symptoms have receded, and the child and his parents feel no need for further therapy. Now would be the time for reconsideration of the therapy program, as there are several courses of action that might be followed. The therapist might point out to the child and his parents how resolution of the presenting problem has occurred, if he is able to do so. In effect, he may point out to them how the child has been manifesting a neurotic reaction that for readily or not so readily ascertainable reasons has now disappeared. If the reaction had been related to an acute situation without significant inherent personal vulnerability in the child, now would be a natural time to terminate, as in effect the crisis has been resolved in such a manner that there will not be a consolidation of pathological neurotic patterns.

If there is persistent basic personal vulnerability because of neurotic behavior patterns in terms of neurotic personality traits, then it would be wise to point these out to all concerned so as to help the family make a decision as to whether or not to proceed further in therapy. If the recommendation is for further therapy, it might be wise for the therapist to alert the family to the fact that the obvious rate of improvement is likely to change at this point. Whereas up till now the progress was steady and movement forward was clear, as is the case so often when one deals with neurotic reactions in children, a plateau has now been reached and one can expect that upward movement will be less obviously discernible in short spans of time. This new state of affairs will be due to the fact that they now are tackling patterns of behavior that do not readily lend themselves to change but hopefully may be altered after repeated confrontations.

There is still another way in which the therapist may proceed at this point. He may discuss with the family these neurotic patterns as being vulnerabilities the child evidences and carries with him. As such, these are vulnerabilities which may be tackled in therapy or which the family may wish to tackle on their own over a period of time, specified or otherwise. In other instances, as the therapist takes into account the "big picture," i.e. the family's acceptance of the child as he is due to the fact that they accept without question the child's patterns of behavior, neurotic or otherwise, or due to the fact that the parents are flexible enough so that they can deal with the child anew without encouraging these particular neurotic patterns, the therapist himself may recommend that the family give it a try on their own before the possibility for more therapy is considered.

There is a danger of polarization when it comes to consideration of termination at the time of symptomatic improvement. There are those who raise the banner for symptomatic improvement and nothing more, and there are those who will settle for nothing less than "personality reorganization." Each may be committed to his particular way of viewing "cure" without sufficient thought to substantiate the reasons for his particular stand. Fortunately, the poles disappear and the differences merge if one approaches the matter of improvement in a reasonable fashion. To proceed reasonably would seem to entail a matter of constantly assessing and reassessing the progress of therapy. Above all, it ought to entail a matter of not scoffing at symptomatic improvement as is done when therapists talk of change in terms of "flight into health" or "transference cure," terms which usually carry the connotation of "no cure at all." The fact is that if one does look closely at symptomatic improvement in therapy that is reasonably conducted, he ordinarily will find some positive element if it is positively altered personality functioning that he seeks.

A second natural termination point might be at the time of a negative transference phase that so often may be found around the time of symptomatic improvement or shortly thereafter. These negative feelings may be overt or covert, and it is ordinarily the latter that poses a significant obstacle to continued therapy. The therapist at this phase many times finds that he needs to deal with a child who in effect "seals over" as the negative feelings develop. Most often these feelings are reflected in protests that he no longer needs therapy while at the same time he is convinced that he has no especial feelings about therapy itself or the therapist himself. If he continues in this vein he is likely to begin to isolate himself more and more from the whole process of therapy as he remains convinced of his need to continue in therapy no longer. More often than not the therapist is likely to learn that the child is functioning adequately outside of therapy at this point.

The decision about whether or not to have the child continue in therapy at this point many times may revolve around the child's general level of functioning at the moment. If the child is relatively asymptomatic and his adjustment is reasonably sufficient, the therapist may decide not to press the issue of further therapy too far when the doldrums set in for what looks like a prolonged stay. On the other hand, if the child's adjustment outside therapy is questionable at best or even grossly inadequate, there may be a need to press for getting through this negative phase even though the phase looks interminable. In effect, the therapist in the second situation might be in a better position to deal with the child's protests at this point as a bona fide resistance and as such be in a better position to enlist the child's ability to see it as such. In contrast, in the former situation the reality of adequate current adjustment may make it well-nigh impossible for the therapist to engage the child in exploration of the possible resistances to his involvement in further therapy. Furthermore, it is possible that this child may be realistic enough in his protests against further therapy, as unrealistic expectations of therapy may be the only rationale for unwavering insistence on further therapy.

How does such a relatively pragmatic approach to termination fit in with conflict resolution that many times is seen to be the ultimate goal of therapy? It would seem that the two positions are compatible. Furthermore, the issue at hand would seem to be that of being a rigid doctrinaire or a more flexible realist. Ordinarily a therapist may at least implicitly set resolution of conflicts as the goal of therapy and establish therapy accordingly, that is, he attempts to mobilize the process that lends itself to resolution of conflicts. In effect, he regularly directs the patient toward consideration of conflicts in which he finds himself, as he aims to have the patient tussle more openly with such conflicts so that he actively works toward their resolution. At the same time the therapist appreciates that the child's conflicts may continue relatively unresolved even while his overall adjustment improves. He shows improvement either because of constriction so as to avoid conflict or because he is able to make allowances for his conflicts as he in effect compensates in other areas of functioning so as to arrive at an overall adequate adjustment. The result then is that the child's adjustment improves, his conflicts remain, and the patient insists on termination. At this point the lines may be drawn between such a patient and the therapist bent on conflict resolution as the prerequisite for termination and as the goal to be achieved at all costs.

The therapist can proceed in one of two ways at this point depending upon how he views the process of psychotherapy. If conflict resolution as such in therapy is his aim, as he takes it to be the only assurance of successful outcome of therapy, emphasis will be placed on continuation of therapy at the risk of appearing doctrinaire. Such a therapist need not be doctrinaire even while he needs to guard against such vulnerability inherent in his stand. If on the other hand the therapist views therapy as a catalytic action in which the whole process of introspection for purposes of achievement of ever greater awareness is mobilized, he can feel assured of relatively successful therapy if at this point he has some assurance that he has helped mobilize this process in the child even while conflicts continue. With this in mind the therapist might then call upon the child to view the present situation that includes the fact that certain conflicts remain unresolved even while favorable adjustments have been made and certain vulnerabilities persist. These vulnerabilities most often are personality traits with which the child and/or his parents are relatively comfortable even while they engender "blind spots" or prove to be disruptive intrusions into reasonable functioning.

In reference to looking for natural points at which to terminate therapy, it might be said that such consideration is in order whenever the therapist arrives at a point in therapy where he needs to choose between attempts "to wait out" the patient or "to smoke out" certain affects or conflicts through further repeated confrontations and between assurance that defenses and conflicts have been sufficiently high-lighted. If the latter is the case, he may decide to terminate with enlistment of the child and parent in continued intro-spection and confrontation that was begun in therapy. The idea would be that in this manner the child would be aided to gain ever greater access to defended affect and/or conflict and that further therapy would be considered only if this process began to falter.

While what is said above may be simple enough, it may be more difficult to get at the spirit in which it is conveyed to the child and his parents. The spirit is that of proceeding in a reasonable fashion in tune with the child and his family and not from an absolutistic, authoritarian position. The therapist can have therapy become a virtual religion to which the patient needs to become dedicated with a fervor while the child and his parents are forced to fit into a rigid mold. Rather the aim ought to be to take into account this particular child and his family with the conviction that there are a variety of life styles, each with its own strengths and its own vulnerabilities. In effect, much of successful therapy would then seem to entail arrival at comfort with one's own life style along with development of ever greater awareness of the assets and the vulnerabilities contained in this way of life. The aim is not to get the patient to conform or to reform himself but to live more reasonably with himself and others. There is no denying that the therapist who proceeds in this manner can be basically paternalistic and authoritar-ian, though in an especially subtle fashion. It is hoped, how-ever, that this sort of approach becomes ever more the product of a genuine, empathic human concern that follows upon greater maturation and not the product of rigid formula.

Once the decision to terminate has been made, there are a number of factors to keep in mind regarding the process of termination. There is first of all a general consideration to keep in mind. The therapist may terminate with an air of finality or he may decide to in effect leave the door wide open for the future. By terminating with an air of finality, the therapist ends with no promise for future therapy. He may allow that the family can contact him for consultation if questions do arise, but emphasis is placed on termination itself, on a definite, permanent disruption of the relationship with no promise that it might be reestablished in the future. The advantage of proceeding in this manner is that it forces the patient (and the therapist) to deal with the fact of termination, a painful bit of reality that either or both may be inclined to avoid.

To terminate without finality is to stop visits at the moment with the expressed idea that the patient is free to contact the therapist in the future with the idea of returning for further therapy if it so seems indicated. The invitation to return may be an open-ended one or the patient may be told to wait a specified length of time before he seriously entertains the possibility of return. While to terminate in this fashion may carry the risk that the patient will never face the fact of termination, there are times when such termination is desirable and even indicated. For example, if the child has problems in object relationships, with either a need to remain dependent on someone outside his family even though the actual contacts with this person are minimal or a need to deny a need for attachment and the fact that he has had any sort of meaningful relationship with his therapist, the therapist in effect may aim to keep himself intruded in the child's life.

Consideration of termination also ought entail length of time through which to work toward termination—a time to allow for disengagement from the therapist and to tie loose ends together. The length of time for such pursuits will depend upon a number of factors that include primarily the nature of the therapeutic relationship and the manner in which the patient has been proceeding. Accordingly, the more intensive the relationship with frequent visits over a long period of time so as to allow for the unfolding of a multifaceted relationship, the longer the time needed to work toward termination. In terms of specifics, the therapist may be talking of lengths of time up to about three months. Toward the other end of the spectrum of therapy is that in which intensive involvement has not been fostered, such as is reflected in relatively infrequent visits over a period of several months. In this instance the therapist might settle on two or three sessions in which to tie things together with the patient.

As with everything else in therapy, when it comes to this consideration of time to allow for termination, flexibility is in order. For example, there are times when the patient has been intensively involved in therapy that has proceeded for a considerable length of time, but he might also have been in the process of disengaging himself from therapy for some time before the final decision regarding termination is made. In such a case the length of the formal termination phase might be shortened considerably because the patient has already progressed well into the process of termination even before it has been formalized.

There are also a number of other specific issues to consider when the decision is made to terminate. There is the question of whether to phase out therapy on the same schedule or whether to do it on a revised schedule with less frequent visits. The decision depends upon what the therapist has attempted to help the patient gain in therapy. If the emphasis has been placed on the development of greater awareness, it then makes sense to continue to termination with the schedule unaltered, as the aim is to continue to have the patient reflect on whatever he experiences, be it termination or be it other phases of therapy. If the emphasis, however, has been on the benefits to be accrued from the relationship itself, it would then be wise to consider the advisability of reduced frequency of visits so as to in effect wean the child from therapy, allowing him to gradually function more on his own. It would seem that such consideration would be the chief reason to justify reduction in frequency of visits. Otherwise, the reduction alters the previously established emphasis in therapy and, as such, remaining therapy sessions are likely to become a nonproductive holding operation.

The manner in which to conduct the final sessions as the termination date approaches is another consideration. Ordinarily it is reasonable to continue essentially as previously. The one change might be to have the patient review what he thinks he has accomplished in therapy, with an aim toward helping him further integrate these gains.

A phenomenon to be anticipated at the time of termination is a return of symptoms for which the patient originally came into therapy. When they do return, they ordinarily can be expected to be of lesser intensity than when originally manifested. Furthermore, one can expect them to disappear as feelings about termination are resolved. If one were to find these symptoms to be otherwise, it would behoove him not to prematurely dismiss them as evanescent phenomena generated by the heat of termination. A clinical illustration of such a return of symptoms is seen in the therapy of Robert, who was referred for therapy at age nine when he and a friend stole money from a nearby home and he identified himself by the name of an acquaintance when apprehended. During the ensuing two years of therapy, stealing was no problem until three weeks before the termination date. Robert was then apprehended for stealing matches in a grocery store, and this time he again identified himself falsely, using the name of the brother of the earlier maligned acquaintance.

Return of earlier symptoms or eruption of new symptoms may rightfully cause the therapist to pause, but it ought not lead to hasty decisions to postpone termination. Generally it is wise to terminate as originally decided if sufficient thought has been given to the plan for termination. The fact is that turmoil over termination is to be anticipated, and when such turmoil manifests itself it is to be handled as one ordinarily deals with turmoil during the course of therapy. Only if this turmoil is not resolvable during the course of termination so that it militates against a successful outcome, ought one to consider the possibility of postponement of the termination date.

V

FAMILY CONSIDERATIONS

How IS OR HOW MIGHT John's parents be involved in his emotional problems? To the extent that they are involved, what sort of therapeutic interventions, if any, are in order for them? These and similar questions emphasize the need for the child therapist to evolve for himself a conceptual framework within which to understand his child patient, and this child's family. More specifically germane to our discussion at the moment, the therapist will need to fall back on his own conceptual framework to plan and carry out a plan for therapy. In these deliberations it is easy enough for the child therapist to become hamstrung by taking an entrenched position on one side or other of the "nature-nurture" controversy. For those so inclined, the lines are clearly drawn. On the one side, and perhaps the more heavily populated one, are those who for all practical purposes see the child as literally the product of his environment. They in effect deemphasize the constitutional factors. They are also inclined to emphasize or to put a premium on the interactional factors in comparison to the intrapsychic factors. When he translates his assessment into therapeutic action, such a therapist directs his energies toward treatment of the parents or the family as a unit. On the other side is the therapist who essentially looks on the child as an isolated unit. As such, he either emphasizes the hereditary, constitutional factors or the intrapsychic factors over the interactional determinants. Such a therapist directs his energies toward treating the child alone. If he works with the family he does so primarily to help them understand the child and his particular disorder or to help them see how the child may be attempting to elicit particular patterns of interaction from them. In any event, the onus is on the child.

Still another position is available, however. The therapist may find himself assuming a paradoxical stance as he deals with children in therapy. When it comes to understanding the development of this child's problems, he may conceptualize their evolution in terms of interactional elements. So the hysterical individual is visualized as having suffered in the earliest stages of development traumatic experiences that have embedded feelings of insecurity and conflicts over dependence. The compulsive is viewed as having been traumatized in his interactions during the anal stage so as to have developed fixations at this level of development. Yet when it comes to therapy, he may find himself treating the child primarily in terms of intrapsychic, dynamic formulations which do not entail involvement of the family in therapy. Such an approach need not be contradictory though it could be. If paradoxical but realistic, it reflects the realization that the child early develops his own personality which is relatively independent so that his behavior then becomes dictated by inner motivations and is not strictly a reaction to environmental forces. Put in another way, though the family may have been intimately involved in the genesis of the child's personality with its neurotic distortions, the same family may not be intimately involved in perpetuation of that which it helped to evolve at another time in its life history.

The aim is not to have the therapist draw camps and for him to pledge his allegiance. To do so leads to rigid approaches to children and their families. Rather, the three approaches listed might be viewed as parts of a total approach to assessment and therapy of children. If he is to choose from options when it comes to therapeutic plans, the therapist must be able to see how the problems can be viewed within several frameworks. Even more basically, however, as the therapist tries to view the child both in relationship to himself and in relationship to others, he needs to isolate for himself the various personal and interpersonal dynamics on which he is to base his therapeutic plans.

Concerning the investigative attitude with which the therapist approaches the family, he first strives to tap the general emotional climate in which the child is raised. To what extent is it generally a clear, invigorating emotional air that enhances development and to what extent does it tend to become an emotionally contaminated one which stultifies or dictates development? To what extent is it a climate that allows for free, spontaneous development of individual potential and to what extent does it tend to become one that encourages or even demands certain types of emotional development, especially maladaptations that are bred of identifications with rigid patterns of behavior? Second, what are the specific interactional patterns to which the child is not only exposed but of which he must become a part? A number of such patterns have been described. There is Bateson's "double-bind" pattern that serves to evoke confusing emotional responses that become unresolvable. There is another pattern in Johnson's concept of "superego lacunae." She refers to a process in which a child never does internalize certain circumscribed moral prohibitions because of his identification with certain specific elements in his parents' behavior.

A word of caution is in order since the focus tends already toward the pathological functioning within the family. Hopefully the therapist might approach the family in a more open fashion. He needs to approach the family in terms of trying to understand the overall functioning of this family so as to have an idea of the family's contributions to both normal and pathological development. It is only within this big picture that he ought to isolate the pathological factors and decide whether and how these can be eliminated or modified. Much too often therapists proceed as pathologists who in their preoccupation with pathology come up with a very much distorted view of the family. Only the negative facets are seen. Only the family's weaknesses and vulnerabilities are examined. Little attention, if any, is given to the family's strengths. In such macabre preoccupations the therapist not only derives limited and distorted views of the child and his family, but he also tends to hamstring his own therapeutic endeavors since he does not become aware of important levers that might be effectively utilized in therapy of the child. These levers are ordinarily to be found within the healthy and healthful family interactions.

What is the general attitude with which the child psychotherapist ought to proceed in his actual therapeutic management of the family? It would seem reasonable for the therapist to have two general goals in mind: (1) he looks for the family to provide a stable setting; (2) he aims to help the family provide an environment that nurtures normal development. While the two are obviously interrelated, it is helpful to distinguish between the two for purposes of conceptualization.

The first task then is to aim for an environment that is relatively stable and secure—the usual being an intact, relatively stable family in which the child has a fairly good notion of what to expect and what is expected of him. An intact family by itself would obviously not be in order if, for example, the child lives there under the open or veiled threat that he is to be on his way out if he commits one or another infraction. Emphasis on opportunity for experiences in a family unit have led and perhaps less commonly still do lead to ill-advised foster home placements that eventuate in multiple placements for the child. Though the opportunity to grow up in the intimacy of a family setting rather than in an institutional setting on first glance sounds so appealing, it would seem preferable to have a child grow up in an institutional setting rather than be shuffled from one foster family to another with repeated development and disruptions of relationships that leave their scars on his capacity to develop meaningful object relationships.

With the family or environmental structure defined as intact and relatively stable, the aim is to help this structured environment maintain a climate that will nurture healthy emotional development. What is such a climate? Put simply it would seem to be one that encourages spontaneous emotional responses that lead to reasonable emotional expression and personal interactions. This is an environment in which there is free, open communication among the various members.

In his attempts to aid parents in enhancing the family's healthful potential, there would appear to be one wellspring that the therapist needs to tap, namely the parents' own emotional responses. In effect, we might say that the therapist needs to follow the principle of always being attuned to helping the parents utilize their own intuitive responses to deal with their child. With most parents it is a matter of helping them learn to monitor and modify their intuitive responses with an informed attitude. Actually if this underlying intuitive response is lacking in the parents, the therapist is literally at a loss as to how he can make comprehensible recommendations that the parents can convert into meaningful action. To give meaningful assessments, suggestions, or advice that does not tap the parents' intuitive responses is to approach the family with attempts at magical solution of problems. The "feel" for it, i.e. the intuitive responses, must be available or there is nothing to tap. The alternative is to invite a cold, distant intellectual approach to problems that are embedded in the emotional life and can be unraveled only by going through the emotional bedrock.

As such, the therapist first needs to assess the parents' capacity for spontaneous, free, emotional awareness and responsivity. If it is lacking, he needs to gauge the extent of its absence and to understand the reasons for such lack. Is it a matter of obsessional isolation in specific, circumscribed conflictual areas or is it but part of a universal pattern of behavior—a character pattern in a cold, aloof, distant parent with an impoverished emotional life? The more it tends to the former, the more the therapist can think in terms of sticking nearer to the counselling end of the continuum of psychotherapeutic programs. The more he senses that he is dealing with an emotionally impoverished parent or parents, the more he will need to lean toward having the parents themselves involved in therapy geared towards freeing themselves in their emotional functioning.

A word of caution is in order. Much too often in dealing with parents there is too wide a split between therapy and counselling, as though the two were mutually exclusive in helping the parents. The more prevalent idea appears to be that the parent needs to work out his own problems. It is assumed that once he works out his own problems all will fall in place between his child and him, as he will then somehow know how to deal with his child. The therapist may also assume that a parent who is in need of therapy is a parent who cannot respond to counselling; either he is a candidate for therapy or a candidate for counselling.

Admittedly the therapist may be in a bind of sorts when he recognizes that the child's problems are intimately intertwined with those of his parent or parents. How to untie the Gordian Knot? Therapy or counselling? Actually the two are not mutually exclusive as some may prematurely conclude. Rather there usually needs to be a blend of the two as the therapist deals with any particular family. So even while it appears crucial, for example, that the mother obtain some therapeutic assistance to deal with her depressive reaction that follows separation from her husband, both she and her daughter may benefit greatly from some advice or suggestions. It would be advisable to tell the mother of the value of not sleeping with her ten-year-old daughter and the need to get her daughter off to school daily though she complains of physical symptoms. Admittedly the mother has worked to reestablish a virtual symbiotic tie with her daughter following the separation from her husband and she needs to work out the feelings that have engendered this move, but it also becomes crucial from the daughter's standpoint that there be some immediate disruption of this pathological bind.

Admittedly there are times when parents do bring their

child to see a therapist primarily so that they themselves can get help. An example of a father in group therapy comes to mind. In this instance the parents did bring their son to the psychiatric clinic because of his obsessive-compulsive symptoms that were disruptive of the routine at home even while he achieved very well in school. In subsequent group therapy the father talked openly and with a great sigh of relief about how he finally managed to get help for himself to relieve profound depression that had weighed him down. He talked of how he had been too embarrassed to seek help for himself. He had figured that to bring his son for help would afford him a wonderful opportunity (in his own words) to "sneak in the back door" to get help for himself.

While the therapist ought to keep in mind that the child may be the "emissary patient" for the family, there is a danger that therapists might exaggerate the occurrence of this phenomenon. How often does this phenomenon occur? It strikes me that in the vast majority of instances the parents primarily seek help for their child or openly seek help for themselves to deal more effectively with their child. Some might object to this assertion, as they feel that it overlooks the parents' reasons for requesting consultation, such as the parent's own distress. Actually most of the parents who come for help for their children seem not to be feeling any hurt in themselves. If the parents themselves have emotional problems, these are more regularly char-acterological in nature, and they themselves more often that not have been able to adapt without any major distress. With such a set of circumstances operative, the therapist is at best unduly optimistic if he anticipates that therapy geared toward resolution of intrapsychic problems in the parents will help the parent to make environmental modifi-cations that will be reflected in positive changes in the child at this stage in his development.

Rather than think in terms of mutually exclusive ways of dealing with the family as the therapist plans a program for the parents that is centered around either counselling or therapy, the therapist needs to think in terms of *where* the emphasis is to be placed in dealing with the family. He may then elect to have one person function as therapist and counseller, or he may plan to divide these functions among two or more people. For example, the therapist might consider the possibility of getting the parents involved in psychotherapy with one or more therapists while he himself elects to touch base periodically with the parents to provide counselling as seems indicated.

Regarding exclusion of the parents from any treatment program apart from having them bring the child and having them pay the therapist's fees, there are different schools of thought about any greater involvement of the parents in the therapy of their children. There are those who emphasize the need for parental involvement in therapy of their own while their children are in therapy, and there are those who see therapy of the parents to be the exception rather than the rule. Though it might be assumed that a therapist maintains either of these approaches because he tends to generalize from his treatment of skewed samples of the population, there are some observations that do not bear out this assumption. For example, different analytic institutes proceed in different fashions. Analysts from one institute will talk of the need to keep in close contact with the family so as to have a clear idea of what is occurring in the child's day-to-day functioning and of the need to have the parents in therapy. In contrast, in another psychoanalytic institute the members will emphasize therapy of the child alone with minimal contact with the family, and therapy of the parents is not the ordinary rule.

Are there no guidelines by which a therapist might decide for or against involvement of the parents in therapy? It does appear that the decision (if and when it is a decision rather than the product of the therapist's particular bias) is most usually based on the nature of the child's psychopathology and on his age. If a child is considered to be a neurotic youngster with internalized intrapsychic conflicts, the tendency will be toward primary involvement of the child in therapy. If, however, he presents a psychotic picture, more likely than not recommendations will include involvement of the family in therapy. If the child presents with characterological problems, the tendency will probably be in the direction of therapy for the parents. What is the rationale? With the neurotic youngster it is felt that there is not the current complicity of family in perpetuation of symptoms. Rather the engine has been assembled within the child, and for the most part the child is seeking out his own fuel. In contrast, the psychotic youngster suffers from ego function defects or deficiencies which require him to rely heavily upon environmental support in areas of these deficiencies. Rightly or wrongly, the therapist will more likely than not tend to feel that the parents of the psychotic youngster are intimately involved in this child's inability to develop in the various areas of functioning. It is therefore concluded that if the child is to grow, environmental changes will have to be made so as to eliminate previously inhibiting or pathological influences and to develop an environment that is more conducive to nurturance of development.

When it comes to dealing with the family of the child with a personality disorder, the therapist's considerations will include varying combinations of those utilized in conceptualization of the treatment program of the neurotic child and the psychotic child. If the child evidences a picture primarily of a character neurosis in which the conflict between id and superego is played out in his personality traits and in his interpersonal dealings, then more emphasis may be placed on therapy of the child. Nonetheless, the therapist will need to be mindful of how the family interactions help perpetuate this type of adaptation. If the parents, for example, are virtually patrons of this type of adjustment because of their own neurotic character traits, then greater emphasis may need to be directed toward modifying these parental forces, probably by means of therapy. A clinical example follows.

Tom, a thirteen-year-old boy, and his parents were referred

for psychiatric evaluation by the family's pediatrician whom the parents consulted because of Tom's behavior problems. The parents felt a need to do something about Tom when they learned that he had again been in trouble while the children were with a baby-sitter and the parents were on a one-week trip. During that time Tom had finagled twenty dollars from the sitter to buy things for himself, and he had used his father's power lawn mower to do neighborhood lawn jobs though he had been explicitly forbidden to use this mower. The parents felt that these bits of behavior were the culmination of devious and defiant behavior which to them had become his hallmark over the years.

In the ensuing evaluation Tom came through as an insecure and depressed youngster, but there were some things about the parents which made the therapist believe that Tom's behavior problems needed to be viewed primarily within the family constellation. First, the parents were intensely angry at Tom and were inclined to view him as a willfully disobedient youngster without a conscience. They could not detect any feelings in him though these were very obvious to the examiner. Second, the parents gave indications that they were inclined to anticipate his "bad" behavior and that he would respond by acting accordingly. For example, the parents told their children not to take ice cream bars from the freezer and then specifically singled out Tom to emphasize that they wanted him to stay out of the freezer. The end result was that Tom did raid the freezer for ice cream bars while the parents were away for the evening. Third, it was obvious that they preached to Tom a great deal. In the process they would convey to him an air of defensiveness and even indecisiveness about the behavior they attempted to prohibit. Fourth, they spent much time trying to exonerate themselves by putting the blame for their failure with Tom on school, neighbors, and Tom's acquaintances. In effect, they ended up doing the very thing which they found so irritating in Tom. Because of these various factors, the therapist referred Tom and his parents for therapy geared toward seeing the three of them together.

If the child with a personality disorder manifests marked distortions or deficiencies in various ego functions, again the therapist may need to switch attention toward work with the parents. For example, it may be discovered in the initial evaluation or subsequent trial of therapy with the child that the parents, because of their own psychopathology and/or pathological interactions with their child, unwittingly, actively or passively, do not allow for any other type of personality development.

COUNSELLING

In his attempts to help the parents of his child patients, what options are available to the therapist? First, there is counselling, which in one sense sounds so pedestrian but which in another sense entails much that can involve a very sophisticated intervention. What it becomes depends upon how the therapist defines counselling and how he then proceeds in terms of counselling. Does it entail a process in which the therapist concentrates on giving advice or does it entail a process in which he places emphasis on deliberation together with the patient?

Counselling often does carry connotations of superficiality or authoritarianism. The term may also generate feelings of futility akin to pouring water in desert airs. For any of these reasons the "nondirective" therapist who aims for insight therapy may by simple reflex shy away from consideration of this form of intervention with parents. What a blow to him when a parent euphemistically talks of bringing her child to him for "counselling," as the term "treatment" or "therapy" has its own undesirable connotations for her!

Perhaps it would be more palatable to all concerned if counselling were viewed as one of the methods available for problem solving in child therapy. No, the emphasis is not on authoritarian advice giving. Rather advice may be the end product of a carefully designed procedure between the therapist and the parent. It might be helpful to conceptualize the procedure so as to include the following steps, with the parent and therapist actively involved together all along the way.

1. *A detailed delineation of the problem.* How many times does the whole business of counselling fall flat because the parent and therapist are on different frequencies! For ex-

ample, often what the parent means by "mischief" is worlds apart from what the term conjures up in the therapist's mind. The two need to talk in "longhand" and need arduously to avoid talking in "shorthand," i.e. the parent needs to draw a picture or tell a graphic story from which reasonable conclusions might be drawn in the next step.

2. *Definition of the problem.* The picture is drawn; the *personae dramatis* have been introduced. Some picture of the interplay among the various family members has been painted. In effect, the therapist and the parents have enough information from which to draw some specific conclusions, especially about individual dynamics or dynamic interplay between various family members.

3. *Confrontation.* This may very well be the most crucial step in counselling the parents. With the picture delineated and some conclusions drawn, the therapist confronts the parent with "This is the way I see it," or "It seems to me that the following is going on." This step is so crucial because either it becomes the endpoint or it leads to another step. Confrontation can be the endpoint for two reasons. First, the task is now completed. The parents may have been in need of a clearer definition of the problem with which they are confronted. Now that they have this clearer definition they are in a better position to work out solutions to their problem or to make modifications so as to eliminate the problem. Such a family then is not in need of advice, as is the case in the following.

> The parents of three-year-old Michael were feeling extremely frustrated with Michael because they found him uncontrollable. Bedtime was the prime example. The night would wear on into late hours while Michael would be making his repeated excursions to various parts of the house. They gave up on spankings since such punishment seemed to have no effect on Michael. Now they primarily talked to him about his behavior, but this was to little avail in terms of getting him to comply with their wishes.
>
> There were two factors that were especially touched on in the first interview. It was noted to the parents that they seemed

to deal with Michael's behavior by either coming down very heavily on him or by ignoring his behavior. Second, they concentrated on his manifest behavior without at all tuning in on underlying feelings, such as fear, which seemed to stimulate at least some of his "bad" behavior.

The parents returned a week later reporting that the week had gone very well, apparently as a result of some changes in their approach to Michael. First, the mother tried to be more responsive to the meaning of Michael's behavior. For example, at bedtime she now would read to him and leave his bedroom door open, as she felt that he may have been frightened. He responded by going to bed and staying in bed. Second, the mother begain to realize that she argued too much with Michael about what he was to do. She now discovered that if she firmly laid down the law, he would protest. However, if she remained firm but did not argue, Michael would carry out the desired task in a few moments without incident. As a result of these changes, the parents felt they needed no further visits, as they were confident that they could now capitalize on their new awareness.

Confrontation also becomes an endpoint when there is no meeting of the minds. In this instance the parents and therapist do not agree upon the nature of the problem. How many times may advice fall on deaf ears because a therapist has not appreciated how important it is that he and the parents agree upon the nature of the problem! If there is no such mutual agreement, there is absolutely no further to go. Before any meaningful advice can be shared, the barriers to agreement need to be eliminated. In effect, the task now is to determine the nature of these barriers. Do the parents' "blind spots" or the nature of their particular interaction with the therapist prevent them from accepting a realistic appraisal of their problems? Or is the therapist not all that realistic in his appraisal because for reasons of his own he misperceives the nature of the problem?

4. *Advice.* Once the nature of the problem is determined and agreed upon, the next step (if there is need to intervene further) centers around advice. It is only reasonable for the therapist to proceed lightly at this step if he appreciates how

difficult it is to give meaningful advice in many instances. Again the task becomes easier if the therapist allows it to become a corporate effort between the parent and himself. In effect, he will find that the best advice is the advice that the parents determine for themselves with the therapist's encouragement.

One needs to wonder how often advice given is advice misconstrued or advice ignored because the therapist never heeded the spontaneous reactions of the one he was trying to help. Generally if the parents are to carry out advice in any sort of effective manner it will have to flow from their own spontaneous, intuitive responses that lead to behavior in their own particular life styles. To the extent that this fact is ignored will it be well-nigh impossible to enhance the parents' effectiveness. The therapist may need to remind himself that unless there are spontaneous reactions to tap in the parent, there is no place to go—the road has ended. How can a parent discipline a child effectively if his child's behavior never annoys him or never even stirs some uneasy feelings in him? How can the parent give more "T.L.C." if his child never evokes tender feelings in him? In effect, there is absolutely no place to go when it comes to giving advice if the therapist cannot capitalize on the parent's spontaneous emotions. Conversely, the therapist with insight will discourage the parent from carrying out any advice which does not mobilize relatively spontaneous action that follows his life style. To hear parents express their misgivings about carrying out some advice because they are not reasonably comfortable in some particular action ought to be reassuring to the therapist, as it indicates that he is on the right track with them. Experience with the parents of an extremely negativistic girl comes to mind.

Sue was an electively mute obsessive-compulsive youngster who not only was frugal in her verbal productions for her mother, but she was inclined to battle silently over most of her mother's requests. Many battles centered around cleaning up Sue's room, as Sue stubbornly resisted her mother's continual proddings to complete the task.

Initially the therapist felt it would be wise for the mother to keep her requests or demands at a minimum because of Sue's insistence on doing battle over even the most reasonable of requests. In effect, he noted for the mother that it would be preferable for her to err on the side of infantilizing Sue rather than to demand even age-appropriate tasks of her.

In this regard he encouraged the mother to volunteer to help Sue with the room-cleaning tasks. The mother did have some misgivings about dealing with Sue in this manner but soon did arrive upon helping Sue make her bed each day. She could not get herself to go any further in assisting Sue clean the room, as she felt that she would end up feeling that Sue was winning out and that she was losing. The therapist strongly encouraged the mother to continue to help Sue with the bed-making chore and avoid helping her any further until she could approach further assistance with a different attitude, i.e. "I just want to help you complete this task. I help so as to prove to you I am available to be of assistance to you. Though it seems to you that to do your chores is to lose a battle with me, I don't feel myself in battle with you when it comes to these chores."

When it comes to advice to be carried out by the parents, it is important to help the parents understand that they are to act in a constructive and not in a destructive manner. Such admonition is germane when the parents will need to frustrate or discipline their child. So even while it is essential that the mother not allow her son John to sleep with her any longer or that the parents make sure that phobic June gets to school in September, hopefully they are helped to carry out their tasks in a manner that indicates to their child a spirit of empathic helpfulness rather than conveys an attitude of rejection.

So at its best, to counsel entails a fine art of problem solving in which the parents and therapist actively engage together. Counselling can be viewed as the first in a series of possible interventions available in helping parents. How well the parents can engage in the process of problem solving and arrive at specific advice at this stage will determine whether or not further therapeutic endeavors are in order. If they can assess the problems realistically and work toward reasonable solutions, why consider further the possibility of therapy for the parents? The problem is not that therapists would ordinarily recommend a program of therapy for the parents if such a lesser intervention were successful. Rather the problem is that therapists may overlook the availability of this lesser option as they assess parents against some abstract ideal model of mental health instead of whether or not they can be reasonable parents with their children.

THERAPY

If it is decided that therapy is necessary, there are several ways in which the therapist might proceed on the basis of several decisions to be made. First, is he, the child's therapist, also to become the therapist of the parents? Some categorically shy away from this possibility, since they feel that they realistically cannot treat separate members of the family because of the complexity of the transference and the countertransference feelings that might be evoked. Such therapists refer parents elsewhere. Second, the therapist needs to decide what type of therapy is in order for the parents. The options include (1) individual therapy for each of the parents, (2) conjoint therapy, and (3) family therapy. Ideally the final decision ought to be made on the basis of patient needs rather than on therapist preferences, but there is no denying that the latter tends to become an important determinant.

Individual Therapy

It would seem that individual therapy for each of the parents is usually the least desirable recommendation. When it becomes "the treatment of choice" for most parents, the decision may well reflect a narrow, biased attitude toward assessment of and assistance to parents. First, it may reflect an inability to assess parents in their role of parents rather than in terms of their more general functioning. Such distinction is in order since it does not necessarily follow that a neurotic person, for example, cannot function as a reasonable, effective parent. Second, to stress individual therapy may also ignore that most often the parents themselves are not "hurting," as characterological problems among them are the rule rather than the exception when it comes to isolation of factors that may contribute to maladaptive behavior in their children. As such, individual therapy for each of the parents is hardly the treatment of choice. Individual therapy may be a reasonable first choice recommendation in the following circumstances:

1. Where one parent is obviously "hurting" and his emotional turmoil interferes with his functioning in more areas than simply in his role of parent. In such a situation there is also a greater likelihood of mobilizing motivation for the arduous task of self-scrutiny.

2. Where there is gross disparity between the levels of functioning, such as one parent being psychotic and the other being at a higher level of functioning so that it would be difficult to deal with them together in therapy.

3. Where one parent has his own problems which, though not directly involved in the child's problems, do become indirectly involved. For example, a parent's depression or anxiety may contribute to family tension that disrupts a "healthy" stability in the home.

4. Where one parent is intricately involved in the child's problems because of his own problems. The parents' difficulties may, for example, lead to a pathological identification with the child, to a need to distance himself from the child, or to a need to have little to do with his child.

If individual therapy is decided upon, ordinarily the parent or each of the parents will be seen by his own therapist. Obviously what needs to be anticipated is the resulting mass confusion that may and many times does ensue. The content of the confusion may most likely center around, "But my psychiatrist said. . . ." Hopefully the child's therapist might be in the best position to keep the treatment program reasonably coordinated so that occurrences of such crises are reduced.

Conjoint Therapy

As described first by Jackson and then by Watson, conjoint therapy involves therapy in which the husband and wife are seen together. As might be readily assumed, such therapy lends itself primarily to getting at pathological interactions between the parents. In essence, therefore, conjoint therapy lends itself to therapy of parents with characterological problems. As such, it does seem to lend itself well to dealing with parents of children in therapy when therapy for the parents is indicated, because, as noted previously, they most often present with characterological difficulties.

Family Therapy

Family therapy lends itself to treating those families in which problems center around pathological interactions among the various family members. In such families an individual member tends to evidence little anxiety about his behavior, as the various members are likely to work out and handle their emotional problems through mutual provocative and projective maneuvers. They therefore are in need of repeated confrontations of what they do to one another if they are to become aware of their own individual involvements, if they are to see how each one contributes to the family disruptions because of his own particular difficulties, and if the family members are then to make appropriate shifts in their interactions.

Choice of Therapy

No more has been done other than to merely outline the options available to the therapist when he is to consider how the family can be helped. The aim at this point is to highlight and discuss this decision-making process, since there is always the danger that the therapist may fall back too much on his own particular biases when it comes to arriving at treatment plans rather than tailor a therapeutic program to meet the family's needs. There are different therapeutic options available. Each does offer something a bit unique that is not found in another mode and, as such, becomes applicable to particular types of problems. This is not to deny that the therapist's own style of work is a factor to be weighed in effectiveness of any therapeutic option.

A word of caution, also, to the therapy purists is needed. There obviously is a need to give serious thought in order to arrive at therapy plans, and once a plan is decided upon the therapist needs to stick with it and not change without due reconsideration. On the one hand, there is not to be change just for the sake of change or to satisfy the patient's or therapist's whims. On the other hand, neither should the therapist feel that he made some sort of final commitment to which he must remain faithful to the bitter end. And a bitter end it can be if there is no room for flexibility. The best the therapist can do is institute a particular type of treatment program on the basis of his assessment at the moment. He does not start out half-cocked on a hasty mission, nor does he start out committed for life. The plan is definite but tentative. A trial of therapy is usually in order to help all concerned see whether or not this is a wise and potentially effective plan.

Various outcomes of any therapy plan are possible. Individual therapy of the various family members may prove to be very ineffective so that therapy of the family as a group may be in order. Or along the way it may turn out that it is necessary to institute modifications in the therapy program to fit the needs of the family. The important thing is to meet the task at hand and not be wed to a plan that does not allow for flexibility which in essence centers around availability for repeated reassessments. A clinical example may help illustrate this latter need.

Greg was a chronically anxious and depressed youngster who dealt with his turmoil by provocative, aggressive behavior that led to insurmountable problems in his interactions with teachers and peers as he entered kindergarten.

After the initial psychiatric evaluation Greg was engaged in outpatient psychotherapy, and subsequently each of his parents was advised to seek therapy. In spite of these interventions,

Greg's difficulties at school mounted. Reassessment at this time pointed to a fantastic amount of tension in the family due to a variety of pathological interactions among the three members. Specifically, it looked as though the parents used Greg as a football in their scrimmages with each other.

At this point it was decided to combine the parents' individual therapy with weekly conjoint sessions to get at the characterological manifestations of their difficulties.

TYPES OF FAMILY PROBLEMS

What are the variety of family problems with which the therapist will be confronted when treating children? One problem derives from a situation in which there is absence of a parent due to death, divorce, or employment that keeps the parent and child apart for prolonged periods of time. What to do about a physically absent parent may pose knotty problems. To what extent is it wise to make attempts to directly introduce a person with whom the child can identify, such as to engage the help of the Big Brother program? Weighed against this consideration is determination of the availability of persons in the child's environment—siblings, relatives, teachers—with whom the child has an opportunity to identify and of whom the child *does* already avail himself. If the father is absent a great deal because of his employment, what sort of modifications, if any, need and can be made to increase his availability? Before he suggests remedies, it would also be wise for the therapist to determine how much it is, for example, the father's absence because of employment that causes a problem and how much the problem may actually result from the father's lack of availability when he is physically on the scene.

Though the parents' physical absences are obvious enough and are more likely to be dealt with, it is the emotional "absence" of the parent that may pose more of a problem since it may be harder to recognize and if recognized, harder to rectify. What does one do with the schizoid parent who in his lack of response maintains a distance between himself and his child? Or how about the parent who in his prolonged spells of depression remains emotionally unavailable to the child? There is also the awkward situation faced by the child of the alcoholic parent who is distant when sober and frighteningly affectionate and even unduly "available" when under the influence of alcohol.

With the parents physically present and emotionally available there are a number of disruptive identifications between the parent and the child to which the therapist may need to address himself.

First, there is the identification of the child with the parent of the opposite sex. What in the family constellation may contribute to this process? Various circumstances may prevail. It may be a matter of "identification with the aggressor," in which case the child sees the parent of the opposite sex as an indomitable figure who poses a great threat to him. Such a condition is ordinarily coupled with the presence of a weak, ineffectual parent of the same sex. Such identification with the parent of the opposite sex may also reflect a retreat from painful interactions with the parent of the same sex. The child in this case many times ends up identifying with a submissive, long-suffering parent of the opposite sex. Such a state is many times, for example, found in a family in which one of the parents is an abusive alcoholic.

Second, there is the child's identification with conscious, readily manifest factors in the parents. Thus the child's antisocial behavior becomes less of a mystery when it is discovered that the parents are engaged in similar behavior, e.g. stealing or lying. Such is especially the case when there are characterological identifications between the parent and the child. Under such circumstances it may be found that the parent evidences some behavior which is essentially the same as his child's behavior which he detests. So the parent who complains that her child lies and constantly blames others for his transgressions may in an interview prove to be very devious and may spend much of her time telling how friends and teachers have corrupted her son.

Third, there is the child's identification with unconscious strivings in the parents. Specifically, the child identifies with unconscious parental instinctual strivings which lead to the development of "superego lacunae" as described by Johnson. In effect, the child is never exposed to clear-cut, consistent prohibitions against certain bits of behavior. As a result, since he does not internalize prohibitions against particular behavioral expression of impulses, he suffers from defective superego development in this regard. To the extent that the parents get "hooked" on the child's behavior as they vicariously satisfy their own wishes, to shut off this mode of gratification by therapy of the child will stir up painful repercussions in the parents. Their own "hurting" will need to be handled therapeutically if further acting out through other family members is to be avoided.

Fourth, there is the situation in which the parent identifies his child with someone in his own past and then works out some persistent ambivalent feelings on the child, as in the following example.

Martha was a fourteen-year-old girl who presented with persistent behavioral problems. At school she was a disruptive element in the classroom and she achieved little academically though she was very bright. At home there were innumerable clashes between her and her parents, especially the mother, over duties around home, hours to be kept, girl friends and boy friends. In fact, there was little, if any, behavior that did not become cause for battle.

It soon became evident that the mother had a most difficult time being consistent with Martha. On the one hand, she unwittingly encouraged certain bits of antisocial behavior while on the other she became very punitive when Martha acted accordingly. In therapy it was learned that many of the mother's problems with Martha centered around the fact that Martha acted so much like the mother's younger sister toward whom the mother felt very much resentful. Though the mother had followed the "straight and narrow path," she felt she did not reap the benefits her sister enjoyed. The mother resented the fact that she had been unable to attend college, while her sister, who had acted up much like Martha currently was behaving, was given the opportunity to go to college. The mother also resented the fact that her sister enjoyed a more affluent life, as she married a successful professional man while the mother married a "lowly" craftsman.

Fifth, there is the parent's identification with his child via particular conflicts. Such identification occurs either through real problems that the child evidences or through problems that the parent imagines him to have. In either event, the parent ends up very much absorbed in his own conflicts so that he remains unavailable to the child who is in need of assistance. An example of such parental identification with a child through real problems is illustrated in the interaction between Mark, an extremely phobic child, and his mother, who was at least as phobic as Mark. She repeatedly fostered and nurtured his phobic stance in the following manner:

> Mark came home from day care trembling with fear after he simply had taken a good view of the "quiet room" which he discovered was used to isolate children who went out of control while in the day care program. When he shared these fears with his mother, she shared with him the intense fears she experienced in small, dark rooms. As a result the two were engaged together in a "trembling session" when the mother more reasonably might have been available to help Mark deal with his fears at the moment.

Another example is seen in the reality-testing problem posed as follows.

> Tony was a borderline psychotic ten-year-old boy who had much trouble distinguishing between fantasy and external reality. One day at home he expressed much fear that men were coming from outer space to invade his home area. Tony's mother tried to reassure him that no such men had arrived. When he remained persistent in his belief, the mother became even more unable to reassure him or set him at ease because "we can't be sure that there are not some men out there in space."

The identification through imagined problems manifests itself in a similar manner. However, in this situation the parent manufactures in his own mind a problem that does not already exist and in the process prepares an environment that will be likely to generate the imagined problem, as in the following example.

> Mary was a twelve-year-old girl who presented with asthma that was found to entail many emotional components. Specifically, she did evidence many characterological problems that included a "sticky," virtually symbiotic tie between Mary and her mother. In interviews the mother's hovering, controlling attitude toward Mary was most prominent as she consistently volunteered to be the spokesman for Mary who sat back in a sullen silence.
>
> One of the main things that concerned the mother was the "poor relationship" Mary enjoyed with her father. Mary's mother portrayed the father to be an impatient, explosive man from whose rage she protected Mary. On further assessment, however, it became obvious that the father was a fairly reasonable man who did not evidence the explosive potential attributed to him. In fact, he was miffed by his wife's erroneous conclusions. The mother's concerns became more understandable when it was subsequently learned that she had had a miserable time with her own father who in fact was the sort of man whom she pictured her husband to be. In her avowed attempts to make sure that Mary would enjoy a better relationship with her father, the mother unwittingly was establishing the very type of "poor relationship" she so diligently attempted to offset.

Actually in the different manners illustrated above, the child may end up identifying with one or both parents via a variety of ego and superego functions. Such identifications obviously are part and parcel of the whole process of normal development and lead to "healthy" growth when the mature parent can reasonably follow through on "I'm going to help my child accomplish some of the things I might have done." However, when conflict and immaturity prevail in the parent's interaction with his child, unwittingly the very thing to be avoided becomes the thing realized and the very thing to be accomplished becomes the millstone around the child's neck.

Apart from such problematic identifications between parent and child, there are other disturbances in object relationships that are likely to generate difficulties. High on the list is the problem of the parent who is unable to let his child individuate. Such, for example, is the case with the markedly ambivalent parent who handles his angry feelings by adopting an overprotective attitude. He then "protects" his child from the anger of anyone and everyone onto whom he has projected his own angry feelings. This is one of the ingredients frequently found in the school-refusal syndrome in which both child and parent are in collusion because of unresolved symbiotic ties. The parent may also be unable to let his child individuate because he is shackled with any of a variety of other disturbances in his object relationships, e.g. unresolved dependency strivings or a sadomasochistic orientation, in all of which the parent needs to maintain a close, sticky tie with his child in order to maintain his own particular type of emotional equilibrium.

Another type of parent with whom the therapist may need to deal is the behaviorally constricted parent whose energy is directed toward the child because of his own problems in reference to the expression of one or all impulses. The results of the parent's efforts are inclined to become manifest in one of two ways. If there is identification with the manifest behavior of the parent, one will see an inhibited child who maintains an emotional equilibrium by repressive avoidance maneuvers. If, however, such a route does not come easily to the child because of his own particular makeup or if the parents' manifest inhibiting maneuvers are combined with a more covert attitude of encouraging the very gratification they so ardently appear to discourage, then the therapist may find a child who is virtually impulse-ridden.

Akin to the above parent is the "overly stimulating" parent who essentially acts in a counterphobic manner. Feeling that his parents had been too repressive in their excessively modest practices around home, he hopes to allow for more "openness" in his children by institution of a "wide-open door" policy in which modesty is thrown to the winds. Or since he feels that his parents' repressive ways had made him too inhibited, he is all for self-expression. He in effect

separates himself from his children in their expressive
moods and allows them to set their own limits as he sits
back and anxiously waits for the day when they will evidence
some self-discipline before someone is destroyed.

SUMMARY

There are several things that need especially to be kept
in mind in dealing with families. High on the list is the need
to be open-minded in evaluation of the family. This openness
is reflected essentially in going from the data at hand—data
obtained by a relatively objective scrutiny of the family—
to theory, and not in the other direction. To start out with
the assumptions that "a disturbed child means a disturbed
family" and "a child in therapy necessitates a family in
therapy" can bring about nothing but a skewed picture of
the family's level of functioning. Futhermore, assessment
ought not degenerate into a process in which the "good guys"
are to be separated from the "bad guys" with the idea that
treatment is to be strongly recommended for the "bad guys."
Rather there is a need to assess the family so as to determine the following:

1. Whether and how the general level of functioning observed in the family may contribute specifically to the child's
problems.

2. Whether the family contributes to the child's dysfunction, while the child is not directly involved in, for example,
some specific conflict situation in the family. Mary, a five-
year-old psychotic youngster with many autistic features
comes to mind. While in day care treatment, Mary was found
to be a barometer of what was going on at home between
the parents who fluctuated widely in their love and hate for
each other. When mother and dad were at peace and the
home scene was relatively tranquil, Mary functioned in a
more organized fashion and was more and more accessible
to the staff and the other patients. Conversely, there were
days in which she flapped her hands, flitted aimlessly, and

was just "out of it." These proved to be times when the parents were engaged in their "cold war" maneuvers which sporadically erupted into "hot war" skirmishes.

3. Whether and how the level of functioning in the parents and in the family at large may be reactive to or may result from the child's difficulties. Such scrutiny is necessary in both the family that presents relatively trouble-free and the family that is obviously conflict-laden, as either level of family functioning may result from the child's problematic behavior. Whereas a therapist may be quick to conclude that dysfunction in the family is a reaction to a particular child's problems, the positive impact on family functioning by this problematic behavior may elude him. Parents who in effect capitalize on their children's problems or virtually need their children to have problems commonly report, "The only thing we ever argue about is discipline of the children. If it were not for that we would never have a disagreement." A similar situation is found many times with the "black sheep" phenomenon. In this situation the various family members travel the "straight and narrow" except for the "black sheep." He is the one responsible for a bit of the discharge of drives whose pressure is mounting because of the few options available to the family members to handle these drives.

With assessment completed, there is a need for flexibility in planning for therapy and in therapy itself. Such flexibility is manifested in tailoring therapy so that it meets the needs of the particular family. This flexibility, for example, means that not all parents of troubled children are seen to be in need of therapy, and when therapy is indicated all families are not put through the same therapeutic routine; rather the type of therapy is determined by the particular needs of this particular family.

This flexibility also allows for modifications in therapy or changes in therapy modality during the course of therapy if and when they are indicated. This is not to advocate random manipulations of therapy programs during the course of therapy under guise of flexibility; rather any alterations in plans need to be well thought out (ordinarily with the patients involved) and need to be based on therapeutic principles that guide the therapist in his work. Most importantly, this option to change the therapy plans is available to the therapist who is flexible.

VI

THERAPEUTIC MILIEU

A COMPREHENSIVE, well-rounded conceptualization of child psychotherapy ought to take into consideration the milieu treatment of children in a residential, inpatient, or day care setting. It is with this realization in mind that milieu therapy is considered in this chapter. Specifically, the aim once again is to help the therapist take into account this aspect of child psychotherapy as he evolves his own conceptual framework. As such, consistent with the overall tenure of this book, this chapter touches upon the highlights of this aspect of child psychotherapy without any pretence of being a comprehensive treatise on this very broad subject but with hopes of helping the therapist arrive at an understanding of therapeutic milieu which allows him to integrate it into his overall management of children with emotional problems.

The fact is that the availability of a therapeutic milieu is of definite assistance in some instances and of complete necessity at other times in the evaluation and the treatment of children with emotional disorders. The milieu can be either of a day care or inpatient variety. Whereas at times there may be a clear-cut need for the child's placement in an inpatient or residential setting because he can function neither at school nor at home, many times the use of a residential or inpatient setting is more likely to be available though it might be preferable to have the child in a day care setting since he still might be able to function at home while he and perhaps his family are in therapy, but he cannot function in his community school. Furthermore, if one were to proceed in a cautiously conservative manner, as is usually preferable in psychotherapy, he might well choose a day care arrangement over a residential one since it is so much less disruptive of the child's life. Be it a residential or inpatient setting or be it day care, however, the following thoughts about therapeutic milieu are germane.

RATIONALE FOR PLACEMENT

The therapeutic milieu can be used either for diagnostic or therapeutic purposes. Diagnostically there are several reasons why such placement might be considered. It may be necessary to get a closer look at the youngster's psychopathological manifestations, be they of a behavioral variety or be they physical symptoms, so as to clarify one's diagnostic impressions. Or it may be desirable to get a clearer picture of his strengths and vulnerabilities via direct observations in a therapeutic milieu when adequate assessment is not possible through more conservative diagnostic approaches. Or the child might even be placed temporarily in order to see how he is able to function in a more positive or at least more neutral setting away from the known pathological family setting in which he now resides. Obviously, placement for any of these diagnostic purposes might be considered to be a drastic measure and as such is not to be arranged indiscriminately but only after the ordinary outpatient diagnostic procedures are exhausted and diagnostic questions remain unanswered.

While there are a variety of therapeutic results that a therapist might hope to accomplish when he places a child in a therapeutic milieu, the reasons for placement of a child for treatment purposes can be reduced to one factor regardless of the presenting symptomatology: the child is unable to adjust at home and in the community at large, especially in school, and outpatient psychotherapy alone with supportive help of family and school is insufficient to help him adjust more adequately. In this schema there is ideally a progression from consideration of day care to consideration of inpatient or residential treatment only as is indicated, but as mentioned previously, in practice, day care treatment is likely to be unavailable in most instances.

There is one other point to consider regarding the child who definitely needs to be placed for treatment of one variety or another because of his maladjustment. Chances are that this child is a "behavior problem." If he is a teen-ager, there is also the strong probability that he is, or readily could be, adjudged delinquent. Accordingly, it will need to be considered whether he ought to be placed in a training school or in a "treatment" setting. While many consider-ations, rational and perhaps some biased ones, will go into the final decision, it needs to be remembered that the decision may not be an easy one to make and at times it is well-nigh impossible to comprehend why one child is placed in a "treatment" center while another is placed in a training school. Perhaps the answer is for professionals to assure that therapeutically sound principles lie behind the rehabilitative program, regardless of setting.

What might the therapist hope to accomplish with a ther-apeutic milieu? In terms of psychotherapeutic goals, he might have one or more of the following aims in mind. He might consider how the structure of the milieu might provide "crutches" and support to the child with deficiencies in various personality functions. Similarly he may think of how the staff might assist the child, for example, in regards to his faulty reality testing or diminished impulse control. In effect, it may need to be considered how the milieu may need to take over for the child and virtually function for him in areas in which he is deficient.

Even more importantly, the therapist might think of how the milieu can mobilize in the child himself the development of various personality functions that will allow him to establish an inner structure by which he may assume a self-mastery rather than be kept so dependent on external struc-ture. This mobilization will be seen to have its foundation in the child's identification with various staff members. Accordingly, the need for such identification will be appreciated and fostered as attempts are made to assist the child to develop, for example, greater impulse control, reality testing, or even wholesome defensive activity like appropriate repression, a mechanism so sorely lacking many times in severely disturbed youngsters.

The therapist also might think of how the milieu might offer this child an opportunity for greater personality growth by affording him a stable, relatively conflict-free environment. Such may be the need for the child who has fairly adequate development of personality functions but who also has neurotic conflicts that interfere with freer emotional expression. A real asset to be derived from the therapeutic milieu in this instance may be the opportunity for the child to interact with staff members who are able to avoid entanglement in his neurotic interactions that help perpetuate his neurotic patterns. Or as the child works out his problems, hopefully the milieu offers him a chance to exercise his unshackled personality skills.

The therapist might also think in terms of how the milieu might specifically assist in the child's individual psychotherapy. Apart from the assistance in personality functioning noted above, he might think specifically of two areas in which the therapeutic milieu might be of definite assistance in the acquirement of greater awareness in psychotherapy if the therapist sees this to be the ultimate goal. It can be helpful in regards to sharpening the child's observation skills, as it offers him the chance to view himself in his various interactions with others by virtue of the staff's ability to confront him with the "what" of his day-to-day experiences. Specifically, they ought to be able to help him observe how he interacts with others and what sorts of responses he elicits from others. Such assistance may be vital in the therapy of the child with characterological problems wherein interventions need to be centered around helping him appraise the nature of his interpersonal dealings, as this is the area in which he drains out so much of his anxiety in maladaptive ways. Second, the milieu might help the child establish a more optimal regressed position that is essential for therapy geared toward development of mastery through ever greater self-awareness. As such, the therapeutic milieu would be of invaluable assistance in helping the markedly inhibited child become more freely spontaneous and in helping the child with massive, uncontrolled regression contain himself to a more reasonable extent.

Ideally all of the above diagnostic and therapeutic advantages may be accrued from treatment of any particular child in a therapeutic milieu, and perhaps all have a bearing on successful treatment of all children in a therapeutic milieu. However, the emphasis on any one particular diagnostic or therapeutic feature will vary from child to child according to the needs of that particular child. In any event, in order to use the therapeutic milieu in a reasonable fashion, the therapist needs to conceptualize for himself the opportunities afforded by such a setting if he is to individualize a program for a particular child or if he is to maximize the effectiveness of a program for all children.

TYPES OF THERAPEUTIC MILIEU

Keeping in mind these various advantages that can be derived from a therapeutic milieu, the therapist can consider the various types of therapeutic milieu that might be established in such a manner that opportunities to derive these advantages are built into the structure of the program or with the milieu so established that any one or more particular aims might be emphasized. Three particular models for therapeutic milieu might be considered in this light.

First, one can think in terms of a primarily supportive, structured milieu that does not formally include any type of psychotherapy in the program. Such a setting emphasizes the establishment of an environment that nurtures personality development. As such, there is no explicit aim to help the child directly with the resolution of intrapsychic conflict though it may be hoped that resolution of such conflicts may be a by-product of his overall experiences in the program.

A boarding school might very well fall into this category many times.

A second type of milieu setting is one that is established in such a manner that it centers around individual psychotherapy. As such a setting ordinarily entails a complex operation in which a variety of people are doing a variety of things with a given child, it is not only important to coordinate the activities of the various staff members during the course of the child's stay, but it is also crucial that initially the specific functions be delineated for all concerned with the care of the child. For our purposes it is helpful to think in terms of delineation of specific functions for the staff members in the milieu itself and similar delineation of function for the therapist who is responsible for the psychotherapy of the child. The functions with which we will be concerned are those that specifically go into making the milieu a therapeutic setting. It is to be particularly emphasized how the individual psychotherapy of the child relates to the rest of the child's experiences in the milieu. While it is true that ideally the formal psychotherapy merges imperceptibly with the child's other experiences in the milieu so as to form a total therapeutic experience in a well-coordinated program, it is also true that such coordination will never occur unless the various people involved in the therapeutic management of the child have a clear-cut idea of what each is to strive to accomplish.

The functions to be assumed by those responsible for the child in the milieu will include the following. For all practical purposes they are to deal exclusively with conscious material or that of which the child can readily become conscious. This approach essentially takes the form of repeated confrontations to the child that answer the question, "*What* are you doing?" For example, "You're angry and you're arguing again." As such, the emphasis will necessarily center around consideration of interpersonal matters in which the child becomes engaged.

All of the above ultimately leads to the readily observable

dynamics of the child's functioning on the personal and on the interpersonal level, i.e. the staff members in the milieu setting aim to help the child see the "big picture" by aiding him to observe the presence of the various forces that generate his particular behavior at the moment. In this manner they aim to attune him to the fact that his behavior unfolds in orderly sequence, though his observable behavior may appear to be utterly chaotic at first glance. To illustrate this point, the following are comments a teacher might make to a disruptive child in the classroom of a milieu setting: "So once again you come into the classroom talking a mile a minute as you look nervous about something. Soon you are attempting to be in a fight with me about anything and everything—the room's too hot or too cold, the material's too hard or too easy. It sure looks as though what goes on in here on a day like this has got to do with something that started before you ever entered this room." As is readily evident in this example, in the process of highlighting the *what*, the milieu staff is bound to touch on the *why*, at least by allusion to it. As such, the staff member ought to stick with conscious, readily observed motivation while he keeps in mind that to examine motivation is to step into the domain of the child's individual psychotherapy. Rather than proceed into this domain in such a therapeutic milieu, the aim for the staff member ought to be to point the way for the child to his individual therapy, as in effect he stops at the threshold when he alludes to the child's motivation. As such, the milieu serves to enhance the child's individual psychotherapy by directing him to further capitalize on his experiences in the milieu by scrutiny of this behavior in his individual psychotherapy so as to acquire ever greater awareness of self.

The one chief way that milieu enhances individual psychotherapy is by repeated confrontations that help mobilize the stuff of psychotherapy, i.e. experiences that lend themselves to scrutiny in depth with an eye toward the development of greater awareness. The aim of confrontation in the milieu is not to expose the child to his faults and failures primarily to reprimand him, though there is bound to be an element of this and not necessarily an undesirable element, as it can help generate the anxiety that may motivate the child to seek psychotherapeutic assistance so as to be able to change his behavior. Rather the emphasis in confrontation ought to be on alerting him to troublesome features about himself that deserve further psychotherapeutic investigation. This message is conveyed loud and clear when the staff member concludes his confrontation with an unequivocal "This is something you ought to talk about with your therapist." Accordingly, in the classroom example noted above, even as the teacher confronts the child with the steps involved in his classroom provocation, the push ought to be to help the child see that the motivating forces behind this behavior are grist for the therapeutic mill.

The setting also enhances psychotherapy by allowing for and encouraging a controlled regression. Specifically there ought to be a sufficient toleration of emotional expression so as to allow for an unfolding, an attenuated display of psychopathological manifestations in which there is also room for self-observation of his experiences and behavior. Contrasted with such optimal conditions is one in which there is virtually repeated "acting out" and "acting up" in primarily a cathartic fashion so that there is little, if any, opportunity to utilize these regressions in the service of therapeutic investigation.

Lastly, such a therapeutic milieu setting ought to help the child consolidate the gains he makes in therapy. Accordingly, as therapy helps him become more responsive to education—the formal, didactic, curricular variety as well as education in a broad sense—opportunities ought to be available for him to capitalize on his receptivity. Besides academic opportunities, he ought, for example, to find ample assistance and support from the milieu setting to learn to sublimate more effectively. While such opportunities can be built into the structure, it will also need to be recognized that to a large extent such educational assistance and support is based in opportunities for healthful identifications with various staff members.

In such a therapeutic setting individual psychotherapy has its own particular function, but the therapist needs to remember that his particular efforts ought to dovetail with those of the staff in the milieu if the child is to enjoy the benefits of an integrated therapeutic program. In effect, the therapist will need to help the child pick up on his experiences in the milieu and use them for psychotherapeutic gain. There are several things to be kept in mind regarding the content of psychotherapeutic investigation and regarding the role the therapist is to assume if his efforts are to be coordinated with those of the staff members in the therapeutic milieu.

Whereas in the milieu setting efforts are made to stay with conscious material, the aim in psychotherapy will be to help the child get to unconscious material. Accordingly, if the therapist works in consonance with the general milieu setting he will attempt to use the "milieu-tagged" material that has come in the form of confrontations (of which he becomes aware through both the child and the staff) as an entree to material of which the child remains unaware. In a similar vein the therapist helps the child move from consideration of his interpersonal interactions to a consideration of how his own inner stirrings are reflected in those interactions. Whereas the milieu staff have made it a point to stay with confrontation, the therapist aims to go beyond these confrontations to interpretation as he helps the child not only to perceive more clearly the nature of his behavior but also to begin to understand more fully the reasons, the motivations for his behavior, i.e. he aims to go beyond the *what* to get at the *why* for any given bit of behavior. In the process the therapist ought to expand on the dynamics that were brought to the child's attention by the milieu staff in their confrontations, and then if possible he can move on to deal with the genetics, i.e. how the child's particular psychodynamics may have had their origins in previous experiences.

There are also particular ways in which the therapist himself might relate to the milieu staff. It would appear reasonable and even essential that as the one with "the big picture" of the child and with all therapeutic activities ultimately centered around the special relationship the child enjoys with him, the therapist ought to be leader of the therapeutic team. As such, he ought to be responsible for the development of an overall therapeutic plan with a clear definition of functions to be assumed by each discipline or staff member in line with above-mentioned roles. Furthermore, as the leader he ought to be responsible for the coordination and integration of the activities of the various staff members during the course of the child's therapy so that the therapeutic milieu might be utilized in a reasonable manner that assures its overall effectiveness.

The question arises as to whether the therapist is to assume the administrative responsibilities for the care of the child. These include the ultimate responsibility for decisions regarding the child's day-to-day activities, be it privileges, disciplinary actions, or visits if the therapeutic milieu is of an inpatient or residential variety. As evidenced by the fact that settings proceed differently in this regard—in one the therapist is involved in administration, while in another someone other than the therapist is responsible for administrative decisions regarding the child—there must be advantages to both approaches. To divorce the two functions is felt to help enhance individual therapy by allowing the therapist to remain more of a "transference" figure rather than become a "real" person on whom the patient is so dependent in his daily functioning. To combine the two functions in one person, having one person be both therapist and administrator, is felt by others to lend itself to an integrated utilization of the milieu setting, as it primarily does not allow for a splitting off of ambivalence.

A third type of setting is one in which the child's total therapy is "built into" the milieu setting and he does not have individual therapy sessions with a psychotherapist. If types of milieu settings were arranged on a continuum, this type would be found somewhere between the two described above, i.e. the structured, supportive milieu and the one centered around individual psychotherapy. With such a setting one might virtually aim to capitalize on what is seen to be the best of two worlds, i.e. while emphasis will need to be put on a firm, well-organized structure that allows for personality development, features of individual psychotherapy are so built into the structure that it is possible to help the child capitalize on his regressions through attempts at expanding awareness and self-understanding. Rather than rely on individual psychotherapy to accomplish this, when the child is involved in any sort of "crisis" in the milieu setting, the staff member on hand or a select staff member called to the scene will deal with the child and his problem at the moment within the context of Redl's "life space interviews." This approach involves an admixture of confrontation and interpretation, i.e. the staff member aims to clarify the situation at hand in his attempts to establish the reality of the moment, and he then proceeds to get at the why's and wherefore's of the child's irrational contributions to the problems at hand. Furthermore, if one looks on content in psychotherapy as centered primarily around the development of a transference relationship, in such a setting one might think in terms of a child's development of "transference to the institution" rather than development of transference to any one particular person. This is not to say, however, that the child himself will not seek out an individual person or types of persons with whom he might interact in his own idiosyncratic fashion in the milieu setting so as to satisfy his needs according to his neurotic patterns.

If psychotherapy is in effect built into this type of therapeutic setting, there then is a need to establish some sort of balance between regression and progression. To establish such a balance looms as a constant need as well as a constant challenge in any psychotherapeutic work. How much regression is necessary at any given moment if one is to reestablish progression? Or when is it more reasonable either to stem regression or not to encourage it because it offers no advantages or even proves to be detrimental to the child's therapeutic management or to the setting in which he is treated? It might be said that in the type of therapeutic milieu under consideration the emphasis would be on progression over regression, as in effect age-appropriate behavior is expected of the child, and attempts are made to help him identify with such expectations. Emphasis on progression will also be manifest in the manner in which regressions and transference reactions are handled, i.e. the veritable crisis intervention in the form of "life space interviews" that are meant to uproot maladaptive patterns of behavior will tend to choke off regressions. In the process emphasis is placed on the development of more reasonably adaptive behavior which constitutes progression. Similarly, when it comes to handling of transference, ready interpretation of transference reactions as they manifest themselves so as to establish reality-based object relationships will also put the emphasis on progression.

PROBLEMS IN MILIEU THERAPY

Be it residential or an inpatient setting or be it a day care arrangement, there are several potentially troublesome problems that may arise in the management of a child in a psychotherapeutic milieu. There is the problem of what may happen if undue emphasis is placed on behavioral change alone. In such a situation the child may function on the premise that the only way to get along there is by being a "good little boy." While there is no knocking virtuous behavior, hopefully undue premium is not placed on compliance as a measure of "healthy" behavior. Though heavy emphasis on compliance may be conducive to maintenance of a peaceful psychotherapeutic milieu, it may not be in line with sound psychotherapeutic management of the child. Such emphasis would hardly be desirable if it primarily fostered reaction formations, engendered an unduly constricted emotional functioning, or even if it fostered an extreme degree of dependence that very neatly fit into the patient's need for a virtual sadomasochistic relationship.

Another problem centers around an encouragement of regressed and inappropriate behavior rather than a toleration of the child's various behavioral manifestations for therapeutic reasons. This nontherapeutic encouragement may take one of two forms or varying combinations of the two. First, there is the indirect, more passive mode in which staff members encourage certain inappropriate behaviors, be it aggressive outbursts or sexual "acting out" or "acting up," by virtue of the fact that they ignore it rather than openly and directly deal with the child's behavior. Second, there is the more direct, active form in which the staff members openly encourage behavior, inappropriate as it might be, usually because they interpret it to be a sign of emotional freedom. In either event there is the possibility that the staff members involved may wittingly or unwittingly derive vicarious gratification from the child's "misbehavior."

The therapeutic stance for the staff members to assume is one in which they tolerate a workable level of regression with its accompanying behavioral manifestations, i.e. to the extent that it can be utilized in therapy. To tolerate behavior in a therapeutic setting is to deal openly with the behavior, even if this involves a mere acknowledgment that it has been observed, with an eye toward immediate or eventual confrontation and interpretation. Furthermore, for all practical purposes it will be found irrelevant at the moment to view the behavior in terms of good or bad. Therefore, such judgment is suspended in favor of viewing the behavior in reference to its adaptive meaning. Such toleration entails an attitude which may not be readily attained by staff (or therapists), but its absence poses a very real problem when it comes to dealing with a child's behavior in psychotherapeutic management.

Another potential problem centers around the child's need to perpetuate his particular patterns of interaction with others, regardless of how pathological these patterns may be. Accordingly, the child who needs to remain passively dependent or needs to maintain sadomasochistic ties can "shop around" to find the staff members and/or patients with whom he can perpetuate his particular neurotic interactional patterns. The child's need in this regard and the detrimental effects that follow from his continued gratification of this need may pose a real challenge to the management of a child in a therapeutic milieu. To avoid this pitfall requires not only intensive scrutiny of the patient's various relationships but also very close supervision of the staff. If all the staff become aware of how the child may be inclined to use them for his own neurotic ends, his tendency in this regard can be exploited for therapeutic gain rather than have the child exploit it for his neurotic gratifications. Akin to this is the problem posed by the child who splits off his ambivalent feelings as he attempts to externalize his conflicts in this regard. The end result is his division of staff into the "good guys" and the "bad guys," which ordinarily amounts to the "gratifiers" and the "deprivers." With a little active encouragement by the unwitting victims, the child may soon feel right at home as he again sees shades of his dad and mom at loggerheads over him. If the child is also involved in individual psychotherapy, when this problem arises it is likely to take the form of milieu staff members pitted against the child's therapist.

There are other problems that may arise if the child is engaged in individual psychotherapy while he resides in a therapeutic milieu. One such problem is that posed by the child who "acts out" his feelings and wishes with select staff members or with other children rather than deal with his conflicts in therapy sessions. In fact, he may be a relaxed, well-controlled youngster when he is with his therapist while quite a behavior problem in the general milieu program. There are several possibilities. It may be that feelings toward his therapist may have become so intense that in effect they are too hot to handle in therapy and as a result spill over into his other interactions in a disruptive manner. Similarly there may be a spill-over of his regressed behavior from therapy to the rest of his day-to-day living when the therapist could not or at least did not deal adequately with the child's regressed behavior in therapy sessions. As a rule, increasing regression in therapy ought to coincide with increasing progression in the child's everyday behavior outside of therapy. Reversal of this process with the regression evident in everyday life and the presence of apparent progression in therapy or the presence of a universal regression inside and outside therapy demands some very active investigation, as the therapeutic process is likely to have gone awry.

There are also problems that may arise when attempts are made to separate too completely what happens in the milieu from what happens in individual therapy. What ordinarily happens in such an arrangement is that the therapist plans to deal only with the material which the child presents in his individual therapy sessions. He is not especially interested in hearing from the milieu staff what goes on in the child's life outside of therapy nor does he wish to become involved in anything that arises in the milieu setting, as he feels that such involvement may distort his role of therapist. He in effect views the child's therapy as virtually outpatient therapy and the milieu as essentially the child's home with the staff members the surrogate parents with whom he feels no need to establish any regular communication.

A therapist with such an orientation will tend to err to the extent that he ignores the fact that the child needed placement for therapy because outpatient therapy either had not worked or was not felt to offer enough for this child. Chances are that the child suffers from more than a neurotic problem, and as a result he is in need of a more structured environment because of the deficiencies or defects in the various areas of his personality functioning. A more extensive involvement by the therapist is also required many times in the therapy of such a child, i.e. the therapist is likely to find that he needs to have regular contacts with those entrusted with the care of such a child, both to keep current as to the level of the child's functioning and in order to provide counsel for the effective management of this child. Accordingly, in the therapeutic milieu the therapist most likely will find that he needs to deal with the staff for similar reasons. Furthermore, if there is to be an integrated therapeutic program that includes the child's individual psychotherapy, there will need to be a great deal of contact and planning between therapist and staff lest they travel divergent paths which lead to chaotic results for the child. From another very practical standpoint, if the therapist does not communicate with staff members, he is likely to waste a tremendous amount of material which is mobilized in the milieu setting and which could be introduced into therapy in a meaningful manner.

VII

FACT OR FICTION?

ALONG WITH THE DEVELOPMENT of a discipline or institution, there is likely to develop a mythology that evolves from the theoretical assumptions of this discipline and which then insinuates itself into the decision making of those engaged in the particular practice. Many times, unfortunately, there may be but a short step from the emergence of myth to its declaration as established fact. Accordingly, as myth is transformed to dogmatic fact, it is especially likely to dictate action when it may be difficult to arrive at a decision about what to do because of the level of uncertainty at the moment. Such is the situation that can easily prevail in child psychotherapy because of the underlying hypotheses that are not easily testable and because of the uncertainty that many times surrounds the assessment of children and family. There may be the uncertainty in the assessment of behavior because of its mutliple determinants that need to be taken into account, and there may be the added uncertainty experienced by the unseasoned practitioner.

Accordingly, the child psychotherapist must constantly guard against the temptation to be lulled by the attraction of unestablished facts which manage to become enshrined in hallowed ground upon which one is not to trespass. If he does question these virtual articles of faith, he may run the risk of being considered iconoclastic and hopelessly naive. On the other hand, if he succumbs to the allure of such manufactured certainty, he is likely to lay aside the indispensable tool of the child psychotherapist, his ability to be skeptical, to look beyond the "accepted as fact" so as to more fully understand the nature of behavior, be it his own or that of his patient. With these things in mind, in the following pages an attempt will be made to review the various questionable attitudes and assertions which may cast their pall on the otherwise reasonable pursuits of a child psychotherapist.

If he is to curtail the insinuation of myth and dogma into his theoretical assumptions, the child psychotherapist needs above all to weigh his own attitudes toward therapy and needs to critically review tenets that he finds he cherishes dearly. At the outset, he needs to seriously consider how he views psychotherapy itself. What value does he attach to psychotherapy? How does he view it in comparison to other methods by which a child with problems might be assisted and his problems resolved? How much does he see psychotherapy offering in the total management of childhood problems? These are difficult questions that may be left unanswered in favor of being lulled into acceptance of attitudes that offer assurance but may be unrealistic. For example, psychotherapists need to keep in mind that therapy alone may not be sufficient. Joselyn notes that "psychotherapy has become the amulet which supposedly has the greatest, sometimes even unlimited, healing value." She sees this attitude as a threat to the future development of child psychiatry, particularly to the future contributions of the child guidance clinic and to community psychiatry. One might take her comments a step further and say that such an attitude poses a threat to the future development of child psychotherapy itself, as it leads to the disillusionment and backlash that goes along with the inability to deliver that which was promised.

There is the real danger that child psychotherapists may oversell themselves as they grossly overestimate their capabilities. Here again the mystique of therapy may shine through as the therapist behaves as though he had the magic amulet. Expectations of psychotherapy become unlimited. The acting-out, delinquent child is to become a well-conforming citizen after psychotherapeutic intervention. The poor reader, the academically retarded child, is to become a Rhodes scholar after he works out his problems in psychotherapy. The point is, however, that even if psychotherapy does have something to offer in these instances, it by itself may be totally insufficient. The child may more desperately need a well-rounded program in which psychotherapy may be but a part. The delinquent may temporarily be much in need of four walls around him or at least in need of a more effective supervisor of his activities. The academically retarded child may be desperately in need of a well thought out educational program geared to help him remedy deficiencies in his learning skills or to compensate for handicaps in the learning process. Perhaps child psychotherapists need to be reminded repeatedly that the child in distress does not live by psychotherapy alone.

Akin to the above, Nuffield raises the question of how effective child psychiatry can be if in effect it takes off in all directions to provide for the total mental health of children and families. The same question could be asked of child psychotherapy. He then quotes some figures that further reflect some questionable attitudes among child psychotherapists. He cites an estimate that some 2,500,000 to 4,500,000 children under the age of fourteen were in need of psychiatric help in a particular year. Of these, fewer than 300,000 were being seen and of those seen, 32 percent received both diagnosis and treatment. That only 32 percent received both diagnosis and treatment does ring a familiar bell, as there is an inclination to emphasize to an unrealistic degree diagnosis over treatment so that we end up with a well-diagnosed population of children who are left to wander in search of therapy. But what about the figures on incidence? The high numbers may reflect a questionable attitude in which the problem child too readily becomes the child in need of psychiatric intervention, preferably intensive psychotherapy if we have a choice. I will say more about this later.

Some might rightfully lose faith in the rationality of child psychotherapy because of the unreasonable approach many times employed in determination of who needs therapy. Others express skepticism about the rationale for child therapy because of the methodically routine input and output that they find, i.e. a ritualized process of evaluation that almost invariably is a prelude to psychotherapy.

In one setting almost invariably the child and family need to be involved in an extensive evaluation that predictably leads to a diagnosis of emotional disturbance for which the child is in need of therapy. Is the process of referral so refined that a child therapist can proceed confidently on the assumption that any child who reaches his office is most likely in need of therapy? Some accuse child therapists of functioning in this manner. In another setting a diagnosis of emotional disturbance and a recommendation for psychotherapy are practically inevitable though the initial evaluatory process is more abbreviated. In either of these latter instances, there will be grounds for skepticism if, as it much too often seems to be the case, the recommended treatment of choice almost invariably proves to be long-term intensive therapy with concomitant therapy for one parent or both. The question arises, Does this profession feel that radical measures supersede conservative management? Or is such management of emotionally disturbed children and their families, i.e. long-term intensive therapy with concomitant therapy for one parent or both, all we have to offer our patients? As such, is to label such therapy either radical or conservative merely a reflection of the bias in the beholder?

Varying degrees of uncertainty are bound to plague a therapist in his therapy with any given child as he attempts to understand the child and the nature of his difficulties. Rather than struggle with such uncertainties, or even accept them as such, the therapist may be tempted to come to premature closure or even to avoid the struggle by calling upon diagnostic labels that make him sound profound even while they add nothing to true understanding of the problem at hand. In this vein, global diagnostic comments like "he's really sick" or "he's obviously borderline" (or even "out and out psychotic") may become favorite utterances when the therapist is confronted with problems that defy explanation and understanding at the moment. To use labels in such fashion may be especially tempting when the therapist deals with a child with behavior problems. Such labels at this time may be attractive on several grounds. Though in reality they are more of a substitute for understanding, they may serve as effective masks of ignorance. "He's really sick" or "he's obviously borderline" may also be said with significant affect so that such a diagnostic label becomes a professional way to set in his place the child who provokes and definitely evokes strong feelings, be it anger or a variety of other feelings. In the process the therapist may also succumb to the fashionable tendency to call yesterday's bad boy today's sick one.

The end result is that the above factors used in consonance may interfere with a truly reasonable approach to children with behavior problems. As noted in an earlier chapter, the fact is that it is not an easy task to deal clinically with a child's behavior and misbehavior in a truly reasonable fashion. While it is to be encouraged that the therapist view the child's behavior within the model of sickness versus health, as it offers a useful framework for therapeutic endeavors, he also needs to appreciate the limitations of this model. For example, it is easy enough to espouse that all delinquent behavior or even all misbehavior be viewed as sick, as to varying degrees such behavior is ordinarily a reflection of emotional turmoil; however, to concentrate on this aspect of behavior may defy both social and psychological reality.

To toss labels about freely may even introduce destructive oversimplifications into the management of the child. For example, it may reflect a lack of appreciation that socially there is something to be said for taking the stand that a child is relatively reasonable and able to be responsible for his behavior relative to age unless proved otherwise. In addition, to label the misbehaving child as sick may be but a short step to optimistic contention that psychotherapy is the answer to management of such children, with the danger that once again more is promised than can be delivered. The error in such an approach ordinarily lies in placement of an undue emphasis on emotional conflicts and the symbolic nature of observed behavior while inadequate attention is paid to deficiencies in various personality skills. Realistically, hope for correction of these deficiencies lies primarily in remedial patterning experiences that include a more comprehensive rehabilitative program than psychotherapy alone. From the therapist's standpoint, to label quickly within the sick model when confronted with behavior may hinder rather than enhance his ability to view the involved child in a truly tolerant fashion. For example, to mouth "sick" or "psychotic" when confronted with grossly reprehensible behavior may be to "cop out" when faced with one's own reactions and/or the need to be involved in placement of a child, for example, in a training school which will essentially be construed to be punishment for the offender.

While there is need for the therapist to guard against the above noted tendency to assign diagnostic labels too readily, he also needs to avoid the tendency to become unduly cautious regarding his diagnostic impressions and treatment plans. This tendency is characteristically manifested in the oft heard "We need more information," which certain therapists are inclined to voice in response to questions about the nature of a child's problem or regarding management of a child. There is much to be said for thoroughness in assessment, but what constitutes thoroughness or completeness in assessment of a particular child and his family is another matter. The thoroughness or completeness is and ought to be relative to the problem at hand, i.e. the therapist inquires and assesses as much as he needs to in order to acquire an understanding that will allow him to make the necessary decisions. To proceed with this attitude is a far cry from becoming slave to ritualistic assessment practices that include for each and every child a specified number of diagnostic interviews and specific diagnostic procedures under the guise of being thorough.

How much information or data does the therapist need? As a general rule, he needs enough to get a picture of the intrapsychic and interpersonal dynamics. An overview of the possible genetic factors helps round out the picture. To get such a picture, however, is much more dependent upon the nature of the data rather than on the quantity, i.e. the data comes from an appraisal of the patterns of behavior and interactions, an attentiveness to how the parents and child say and do things rather than exclusive concentration on what is said or done, or on what has been said and done. (More has been said about this in Chapter II.) Accordingly, in fairness to those who oft repeat, "We need more information," more often than not they probably are saying, "We need different kinds of information"; information that will spell out dynamic interplay rather than merely catalogue happenings. However, to say, "We need more information," and mean it literally can be a familiar ploy when the going gets tough, such as when there is an unpleasant decision to be made. An illustration is seen in the following clinical example.

Psychiatric opinion was requested regarding whether the natural father ought to visit his children in their foster home. His children consistently were very much distraught for several days after disruptive visits with him, and there was no getting the father to change his unreasonable practices. The psychiatrist who was called in on consultation saw the children, weighed the situation, and recommended that the father's visits be sharply curtailed. The involved agency had some reservations about the recommendation because its implementation would not be an easy task. Their next move was to order psychological testing, and they postponed a decision on alteration of visiting plans until they "learned from the tests if and how continued visits would hurt the children." It was very difficult to imagine how results of psychological tests could add anything to the picture. Rather the testing itself could serve as nothing but a delaying maneuver when confronted with a need to make an unpopular and even legally complicated decision.

As in this clinical example, the need for more or different kinds of information many times is not the issue at hand. Rather the issue is likely to revolve around pressure on the therapist to give some specific explanation or to make specific recommendations. In the latter situation, especially, if the recommendation involves significant changes in the child's life, be it whether father will visit, as in the above example, or be it whether the child should be placed away from home, it may be especially tempting to insist that more information is necessary. It is as though getting more information will make the decision easier to make or will make it look like a more profound and more deliberate decision even at a time when one might actually conclude, "But it wouldn't take Freud and his Vienna Council to figure that one out!"

There are times when emphasis itself on a prolonged investigative approach can present its own problems. For one, it can be surrounded by an aura of unduly profound deliberation so that it appears promising and the family expects much more than is likely to be delivered at the end of the assessment. Furthermore, the family may become more passively involved in the whole diagnostic process, as they are led to believe that the most important thing is for them to cooperate with bits of information and then sit back and wait for the deliberations of the therapist or the "team." Wittingly or unwittingly, the impressions and recommendations may then be presented to the family in an unduly authoritative manner so that the family is awed and feels compelled to accept what is told to them, as they rightly or wrongly figure, "With all those high-powered deliberations on these matters, how can I possibly disagree with his (or their) conclusions!" If the family then enters therapy of any variety, the first task may be to educate them to the true spirit of psychotherapy, i.e. an experience in which there is no secretive, behind-the-scenes skulduggery that "forces" people into action but an open, aboveboard interchange in which all participants are free to and need to share their deliberations with one another.

If it is decided that therapy is indicated, there are likely to be heard a number of definite, unequivocal assertions which are especially attractive because they help dispel the heavily hanging air of uncertainty within which decisions may need to be made. In this vein there is the often heard emphatic assertion, "He is obviously in need of therapy!" The more doctrinaire might even specify the particular type of therapy, be it individual, group, family, or any other variety.

When are a child and his family "obviously" in need of therapy? Unfortunately, the answer is not all that clear. The decision could be easy enough to make if one were to base it on particular types of symptoms or on diagnosis of emotional disturbance, but it can also be grossly unrealistic to make the decision on such a basis. While ordinarily it can be assumed that the child and family who present with problems are in need of some sort of help, it is also true that ordinarily it is likely to be found that psychotherapy of any particular variety is but one option among several that might be employed to help resolve the problem at hand. While psychotherapy might be a reasonable choice, to present it as the lifeline upon which continued existence depends is yet another matter, especially when it is offered in this manner without due attention to other options available to ones in distress.

Such dogmatic assertions about the obvious need for psychotherapy are a problem primarily because they ordinarily become a poor substitute for a reasonable approach to the family and to the problem at hand. If there is an obvious need for therapy, this is a decision at which both the therapist and the family ought to arrive at the end of their deliberations together rather than a decision imposed upon the family from the authority on high. Ordinarily the most reasonable way to proceed would be to discuss with the family the nature of the problem(s) at hand and the possibilities for their dealing with the problem either by themselves or with outside assistance. Even if it seems more clearly indicated that they obtain professional assistance, it usually does remain for the family to decide how much they are interested in such help or whether they might prefer to try other ways to handle the problem. The main point is that the family is to be intimately involved in the process of making a decision regarding psychotherapy, especially since the meaningful coercion for involvement in therapy comes from personal conviction as to the value of this endeavor. Furthermore, again the therapist needs to remember that there are ordinarily a number of options from which one might choose in dealing with a problem, psychotherapy being but one of them.

There is also the danger that the therapist can become so enamored with psychotherapy, especially a particular variety of psychotherapy, that he does not see how in a particular situation it might be more disruptive than helpful. The following clinical examples come to mind.

> A four-year-old boy had already been in and out of several foster homes in two years because he regularly was found to be too aggressive and destructive. It was now decided that he be seen for psychiatric treatment regarding his apparent difficulty in establishing meaningful relationships and that he also be placed with an experienced foster mother who had been successful with a variety of foster children. However, what also needed to be considered was the possible impact of the boy's relationship with the therapist on the relationship he had begun to establish with his foster mother. One could have argued with merit that the boy's experience of a satisfying relationship with his foster mother was exactly what he needed and that it would be in this relationship that he could work on his fears of investment in people. In this light, the relationship with a therapist at this time would likely be disruptive because of its possible dilution of what was going on between the child and his foster mother and because of the additional strain on their relationship due to feelings of rivalry between stepmother and therapist which were likely to develop.

> A seven-year-old boy presented with encopresis within a year after his father remarried. The boy's natural mother had died when he was about three, and in the evaluation it was clear that emotionally he had never come to reasonable grips with his mother's death. It appeared that therefore he was having considerable difficulty establishing a meaningful relationship

with his stepmother. However, there were also indications that emotionally she was not set for the task of helping him work things out between the two of them. The decision, however, was to involve this boy in individual psychotherapy to help him resolve conflicts that interfered with his ability to establish a meaningful relationship with his stepmother. Again, one could also build a strong case for at least initially concentrating therapeutic efforts on the relationship between the child and his stepmother with both involved in a commonly shared therapeutic endeavor. Might not a relationship with a therapist only further establish a rift between child and stepmother at a time when it might be more desirable to force interactions between the two of them and from which they might be helped to forge a mutually satisfying relationship?

In both these clinical examples, the therapists fell back on the commonly held thesis that it might be desirable to have the child work out his problems in a therapeutic relationship with the hope that subsequently he might engage more meaningfully with his parents. While this rationale is sound when dealing with firmly established patterns of behavior so that one needs to undo and restructure patterns, it would appear that with children such as those in the previous examples, there is the matter of patterns still being established. Therefore, rather than emphasize an undoing and redoing, one needs to think of how he might intrude in such a manner as to modify and structure, since a certain degree of plasticity remains. Accordingly, rather than put the emphasis on working out problems in a contrived relationship as in therapy, one aims to help such a child work out his problems through investing and while investing in his ordinary day-to-day relationships.

When therapy is said to be obviously necessary, it many times is so proposed with the added stipulation that this child and his family are ideal candidates for therapy at another mental health center or with particular private practitioners down the street or across town. The more emphatic such assertions, the more skeptical one needs to be about such referrals. While reasons for referral for therapy may sound plausible enough, they can readily become a rationalization for referral of undesirable patients. And undesirables there are in terms of children with extremely complicated problems who are involved in impossible home and general environmental situations that require at least the wisdom of a Solomom to unravel and infinite powers to implement solutions.

Referral is appropriate when it is for a certain type of therapy which the referral source cannot provide while the one to whom referral is made can offer such help. In reality, such a set of circumstances does not ordinarily prevail, unless it is a matter of a private practitioner who restricts his type of practice or a clinic with limited personnel or one established to deal with restricted types of patients or to provide a specified service. More often than not, a particular clinical setting is complete in itself in the sense that it is able to tend to the needs of those who get beyond intake and are able to be managed on an outpatient basis. (Admittedly it may be quite a struggle to get beyond intake!) Caution on the part of all concerned is in order if reason is to prevail in this whole matter of referral for therapy. The truth is that so many times a child and his family look like tremendous candidates for therapy—as long as the one who labels them as such is not to be their therapist. It often is amazing how the child and parents undergo a metamorphosis if it turns out that the one who wishes to refer the family elsewhere will need to provide the therapy himself.

If it is decided that therapy is in order, there are uncertainties about frequency of visits that also might be handled by dogmatic assertions. This matter becomes especially true when the therapist thinks of relatively intensive therapy with two or more sessions a week. Does the child definitely need to be seen three times a week? Or is the "definitely" a reflection of the therapist's overly biased view and/or inflexibility? From the standpoint of offering real assistance to the child and his family, rarely does frequency of visits become an either/or proposition. Most commonly, the ther-

apist will strive for more frequent visits than the patient and
his family deem necessary. While there are many neurotic
reasons that may prompt a family to balk, the possibility of
several visits a week does introduce some realistic concerns.
There is the consideration of practical matters like time and
money. Whether or not the financial burden is a potential
problem, time can be a major consideration. It can be very
much disruptive of the child's life to have him make two or
three visits a week to a therapist. Accordingly, the therapist
may need to weigh seriously the advantages to be gained
in such therapy versus the disadvantages likely to accrue
from his not being able to engage in his usual activities. Do
the advantages to be gained from therapy in a given instance
justify the child's regular absence from a certain class if
the therapist's schedule demands such absence? Or do the
advantages justify his forced lack of involvement in extra-
curricular activities? In another instance, what impact does
the investment of substantial time in the child's therapy
have on the rest of the family? While there are times when
one can build a strong case for insistence upon a need for
either frequent visits or none at all, there are many times
when the eventual schedule can realistically be a compromise,
i.e. while the therapist proposes a schedule that would allow
for goals ideally to be attained, practical considerations may
dictate otherwise.

The therapist may also maintain with some legitimacy
that he needs to establish with the family from the onset
that he is not to be manipulated by their whims, such as in
regards to frequency of visits. There may be the possibility
that the family's stand is a reflection of manipulative attempts, but even if it is, why be all that concerned unless
there is involved unreasonable compromises by the therapist?
The more a therapist becomes experienced, the more he
is likely to find that preoccupation with fears that the family
may attempt to manipulate is likely to be a mark of a therapist's insecurity or naiveté. The fear of being manipulated
by children and parents may reflect a therapist's need to

be authoritarian, a need therapists ordinarily wish to disavow but which may become evident in feebly rationalized, semilegitimate stands they assume with families. In actual practice, the therapist is more likely to discover that such compromises with families about the frequency of visits and the goals of therapy need not interfere with effective therapy. It is true that they may preclude engagement in the type of therapy the therapist would ideally like to pursue, but they can also bring about therapy that more appropriately suits the needs of the child and his family. There is something to be said for allowing the child and his family to have a voice in the decision about goals toward which to strive and the road to take toward attainment of these goals, if there is more than one possibility in these regards, as is the case so often in therapy planning. If the therapist can leave himself open enough to the unexpected, he may find that some children and families are able to make remarkable progress under less than ordinarily considered ideal schedules, i.e., seeing the patient once a week rather than two or three times a week.

If the child is to be engaged in therapy, there may be the question of therapy with whom. This decision, too, may be made to sound like a learned, scientifically derived one though there actually may have been meager reason to take an absolute stand. Accordingly, it will be heard, "This child definitely needs a male therapist and that one definitely needs a female therapist." For example, some therapists will be quick to conclude that the adolesecent girl needs a woman therapist because she may be unable to tolerate positive feelings in her relationship with a man therapist, especially if he is relatively young. Or it is argued that the child needs a therapist of the same sex with whom to identify if it is felt that the benefits of the relationship itself are to be emphasized and exploited in the therapy.

It is true that the adolescent's rapid development and involvement in transference feelings can pose a very real problem in therapy. For example, the adolescent girl in therapy with a man may quickly become engulfed in positive feelings that frighten her and make her feel vulnerable. Her ensuing defensive maneuvers are likely to include tremendous negative feelings that may seriously interfere with her ability to become involved in intensive therapy geared toward development of greater awareness. However, it is also true that the girl who gets so quickly involved and so quickly threatened in her therapy with a man is likely to become similarly involved and threatened if she sees a woman therapist. (These considerations are also applicable to the adolescent boy in therapy.) Accordingly, whereas discussion may center around whether this particular adolescent should see a man or a woman, it would be more appropriate to think in terms of who will be able to deal skillfully with him or her. Specifically, the therapist will need to be very much attentive to the nature and the extent of the patient's involvement and be ready and able to deal with the transference reactions so that the patient is not quickly "over his head," panicky, and beyond the therapist's helpful reach. It is especially noteworthy that a skilled therapist, man or woman, can deal with a wide variety of patients of either sex. As a result, rarely, if ever, does it appear that one can categorically say that a particular patient definitely needs a man therapist or a woman therapist because of the types of reactions that are likely to unfold. A skillful therapist, yes; but a therapist of a particular sex, maybe, at best.

Similarly, when "relationship therapy" is emphasized for a particular child, it is likely to be said that the child needs a therapist of the same sex with whom he might identify. As such, identification is seen primarily in regards to gender, and it is at least implicitly assumed that the identification which is sought is to follow from identification with a person of the same sex. If this assumption is correct, there is another factor to consider. As the child scheduled for "relationship therapy" most usually is likely to be from the culturally deprived, lower socioeconomic group, it may be overlooked that a man as therapist or a woman as therapist may not fit with or may even be in opposition to what constitutes a "real" man or a "real" woman in the child's environment. More importantly, the sort of identification desired is likely to involve identification with an approach to oneself and to problems in life—an approach that generally involves attempts at greater self-mastery and as such is not tied to gender. The availability and the approachability of the therapist would therefore appear to be more crucial than his sex.

There are also articles of faith or myths upon which the therapist may fall back when he needs to consider the possible involvement of the child's parents in therapy. "Obviously the parents both need to be seen and ideally each ought to be involved in individual psychotherapy." "Obviously the parents better be seen together by a therapist other than the child's therapist." "Obviously the mother also needs to be seen in intensive psychotherapy." However, on closer scrutiny the obvious so many times becomes hardly so discernible. In fact, closer scrutiny may reveal that the decision is based more on ritualistic practices that are derived from questionable assumptions about these parents or about parents in general. As such, the therapist may be hardly attentive to the needs of this child and his parents. There are some who place a taboo on having the same therapist see a child in individual therapy and concurrently the child's parent or parents in counselling or modified psychotherapy of one variety or another. The usual reasons given for taking this stand are that such an arrangement "fouls up" the transference and that it may interfere with the child's ability to confide in his therapist. More specifically, it is felt that the child may become inhibited in therapy out of his fear that the therapist may side with his parents and may even divulge "secrets" of therapy to his parents.

Admittedly, the child's relationship with the therapist does become a more complicated one when the therapist elects to see a child and his parents concurrently, though the nature and the frequency of visits of the two are different. However, if the therapist elects to see both the child and the parents, chances are that the nature of the child's problems is such that resolution of them through therapy geared toward attainment of a relative transference neurosis is not feasible, i.e. chances are that the child is not an essentially neurotic youngster with minimally disruptive behavior and that he is not a child who will or can bring his problems into therapy in a manner that allows for reasonable solution. Or in another sense the therapist may see that he needs to engage the child and parent(s) in therapy so that he might attend to the interaction between child and parent(s). Because one or more of these factors is operative, to dwell on the possible impact of this arrangement on the transference may involve concentration on the irrelevant, as helping this child may require more than dealing with evolution of spontaneous transference reactions. At the same time, this is not meant to dissuade a therapist from being attentive to transference ramifications. Rather he needs to appreciate not only that distortions introduced into any relationship are in part based on transference, but also that the stance he takes may tend to elicit particular transference reactions. Accordingly, when the therapist also has contacts with other family members, he needs to pay attention to how such contacts may affect the child's relationship with him and be prepared to deal with the child's reactions as they arise.

With whom will the therapist side in his dealings with the child and his parents? As issues do arise among the various family members, the participants may pressure the therapist to choose sides, to align himself with the one who is "right" and chastise the culprit(s). The logical stand for him to take would seem to be that from the beginning he let it be known that he sides with no one exclusively but that he sides with each of them separately and with each of them as a member of the family. Put another way, he is concerned about the general welfare of each alone as well as about the welfare of the family. Accordingly, his acceptance of the person or persons does not mean a total commitment that includes casual acceptance of neurotic distortions in one member at the expense of the other members in the family. More positively, he conveys to them that if he feels a need to side with anybody or anything at a particular moment, he will side with the reality at the moment, the reality which he will always attempt to delineate with them and not arbitrarily establish by himself. Accordingly, they all are most likely to join together into consideration of the interpersonal dynamics. As such, they all are likely to find that there is no looking for the "good guys" and the "bad guys." Rather the task at hand is to look for the manner in which and the extent to which each has been involved in whatever has transpired among them, not to pass judgment on one another but to arrive at an understanding that might allow for each to approach the other more reasonably. When the therapist sees the child and the parents in separate sessions, the issue of whether and with whom he is to take sides also becomes irrelevant as long as the therapist does not allow himself to end up the messenger between the parents and the child— mediator, maybe; messenger, definitely not, for to assume the latter role is to consolidate cleavages. At a given moment it may be that the therapist will feel strongly compelled to convey information from one to the other rather than get involved in the more difficult task of helping establish lines of communication between the parents and the child.

During the course of therapy, the therapist may also be tempted to fall back on ritualistic routines when the going gets rough and the child does not improve as anticipated or as quickly as is desired. The therapist may feel an urgency to have things turn for the better or the family may feel an urgency for more rapid improvement, as they experience frustration and diminished hope due to the lack of progress or even deterioration in the child's adjustment. In any event, the pressure will be on the therapist, who may respond with a feeling that something has to be done and has to be done quickly.

There are several practices that are ordinarily employed

under such circumstances. First, there is the tendency to increase the frequency of the child's therapy sessions with the avowed rationale that the child "obviously" needs to be seen more often. Accordingly, if he has had one session per week, he henceforth is to come twice a week. The child who was coming twice a week has his sessions increased to three times a week. Often enough, little thought is given as to why the frequency of visits should be increased and as to how such increase will meet the problem at hand. It is just generally assumed that more frequent visits will "obviously" help change things for the better. Who is to say that if the child has so much trouble and therapy is so difficult when he comes one time each week that things may not end up two times or three times as bad if the frequency of visits is increased? Such might end up being the case if the reason for the child's deterioration or apparent deterioration is not clearly defined and handled in an appropriate manner in therapy. Another set of ritualistic practices centers around putting the onus on the family if adjustment of the child lags or deteriorates during the course of his therapy. Accordingly, at such times of stress the therapist may feel strongly inclined to say categorically but with little evidence at hand that something "obviously" must be amiss in the family. It then follows that if the parents are not already in therapy, they had better be engaged in one variety of therapy or other; or if they are already in therapy, some sort of alteration in their therapy plan may be seriously contemplated.

There is no denying that changes in the therapy of the child and the parents do become indicated at times. However, such manipulation of therapy schedules and therapy approaches can become gestures which are pointless except as attempts to alleviate the family's or the therapist's anxiety, and as such they are not appropriate at the given moment. When some crisis in the child's adjustment does occur during the course of therapy—and crises do arise regularly in therapy unless the child is involved in no more 'han an intellectual exercise—the emphasis ought once again to be on understanding and not on action. In other words, whatever course of action is eventually decided upon ought to help meet the problem at hand and not merely make the therapist and/or family feel relieved because something is being done. As such, the therapist is likely to find that in the vast majority of cases the most reasonable thing to do is to do nothing other than remain cool, calm, and collected.

To act for the sake of doing something at times of crisis in therapy may even be detrimental on several counts. First of all, the therapist may forget that in many instances he provides a tremendous service for the parents and the child by remaining calm and steadfast during what appears to them to be an impossible crisis that demands immediate action. At the moment it may otherwise be impossible for the family to see that the most reasonable thing to do is to reestablish their bearings and proceed from there. In effect, by his composure the therapist remains the beacon in the storm, the steadying force when the family is ready to panic. Ekstein talks of the need to bide for time, to help the patient and family at time of apparent crisis extend the time span when they feel compelled to constrict it down to a brief moment. If the therapist also pushes the panic button, he is likely to neutralize and even destroy much of his potential for assisting the child and his family. These points can be all the more appreciated to the extent that the therapist appreciates that so much of child psychotherapy does truly involve crisis intervention. To respond quickly to a "crisis" during the course of therapy with a change in therapy plans may be to establish an undesirable precedent or to further establish a precedent which the therapist might more profitably strive to eradicate, i.e. the tendency to act hastily and even impulsively, to quickly try to do something, may already be a problem for the family. If they are to act more reasonably and function effectively, they may need to develop the capacity to assess problems that do arise and in turn proceed more deliberately on a course of action.

Accordingly, it behooves the therapist to avoid making

hasty decisions that involve a change in therapy or the direction of therapy when a crisis arises during the course of
therapy. To do otherwise is to invite trouble and even disas-
ter. Above all, the change may be totally unrealistic, as it
is in reponse to the anxiety of the therapist and not to the
needs of the patient. While it is important that the therapist
maintain some sense of security, hopefully he might accomplish this purpose through greater maturation as a therapist
and through increased knowledge and appreciation of human
functioning rather than through what proves to be a capricious
exercise of power.

While the child psychotherapist needs to guard against
reliance on certain ritualistic practices, he also needs to
avoid being lulled into a complacent acceptance of certain
attitudes which are likely to permeate the thinking of child
psychotherapists. High on the list is a cynical attitude about
a child's improved adjustment as gauged by observable behavioral changes. "It's a flight into health!" "It's behavior
change only, so he's likely to slip back." While these and
similar comments sound especially attractive from a theoretical standpoint, the fact is that such cynical pessimism
is not substantiated by clinical experience. Such an attitude
may in fact unduly restrict a therapist's options with any
given child and his family, as it leads to preoccupation with
pathological considerations and does not give quarter to
attempts at isolation of more specific problems to which
he might tend with the family in a meaningful manner. At
times such an attitude may even lead to approaches that go
strictly along theroretical lines though clinical experience
may dictate otherwise. For example, there are some who
when dealing with the child with a school-refusal problem
will not emphasize that he needs to return to school promptly.
Instead they hold that primary emphasis will need to be
placed on the underlying problem of which school-refusal is
the product. Such an approach, however, goes counter to
the readily demonstrable clinical fact that unless a child with
a school-refusal problem is returned to school quickly, one

can in a very brief period of time end up with a very
complicated problem that defies any sort of therapeutic
management.

Attitudes are also to be questioned when there is too
ready an acceptance of the oft-found fact that it may be
easier to arrange for a child to be placed in residential treatment than to get him involved in outpatient psychotherapy.
While lack of personnel for outpatient therapy may be a real
enough problem, too ready acceptance of this paradoxical
situation often enough is accompanied by questionable attitudes toward management of children's problems. Foremost
on the list is the attitude of looking on a child's problems in
unduly global pathological terms in the sense that the therapist may be too quick to see a child as "very sick" and in
need of extensive "overhauling." As such, it may become
difficult to proceed in such a manner that he primarily
attempts to isolate problems so that in effect he might
serve as "problem solver" or catalyst rather than modern-day
alchemist in the psychological realm.

When residential treatment is recommended, it often
comes as a shock to the parents for them to hear that it
will be a matter of months before such placement can be
expected. The shock is generated especially by an oft-found
mystifying contradication between what is said about the
child's condition and the manner in which he is tended to, i.e.
while the therapist may voice grave concern about the
severity of the child's state, he may also end up very non-
chalant about the interim management of the child while
preparations for placement are made. In effect, the parents
may feel that they are left with a realization that they have
on their hands a monster, even a potentially dangerous one,
or that they are sitting on a keg of dynamite, but nothing
can be done until rescue comes in the form of placement.
While solutions to such interim management of children
prior to placement are not easily forthcoming, there is need
for the therapist to be attentive to the possibly great disparity between the voiced concern about a child's adjustment

and the casual manner in which placement arrangements are then handled.

Child therapists also need to avoid a too ready acceptance of the inevitability of lengthy waiting lists for the examination and therapy of children with emotional problems. Long waiting lists and their ready acceptance are likely to exist especially when certain attitudes prevail. Such may be the case, for example, when there is a premium on lengthy, ritualized diagnostic procedures and long-term intensive therapy over more conservative, more flexible approaches to problems in children. With complacent acceptance of the inevitability of waiting lists there is likely to be an emphasis on planned or unwitting screening of patients away from the diagnostic and treatment facility. The unwitting screening out has been referred to as a "cooling out" (Adams, 1968) process in which obstacles such as lengthy, complicated intake procedures systematically obstruct a family's path and make it difficult for them to proceed so that only the hardy, dedicated and even obstinate persist and gain entrance to the hallowed halls. Such "cooling out" does reflect a tendency toward a general unavailability that may become the trademark of some child psychotherapy clinics and those therapists who espouse a relatively narrow-based approach to the problems of children and their families. While such unavailability many times is meant to serve as a means to hold back the alleged hordes of mentally ill, it may be that in this manner, child therapists may be cooking their own goose, preparing their own demise, at least as leaders of those committed to tend to the mental health of children and their families.

To be reasonably available may not be all that easy a matter, especially if availability is confused with other issues such as the fear of being forced into trying to be all things to all people. The therapist is likely to find that such an issue for the most part becomes irrelevant if he proceeds with an open mind and does not see himself functioning in a too exclusive type of approach, such as reliance on lengthy diagnostic procedures and extensive psychotherapy. If he can be more open in his approach, he is likely to find that there is a broad spectrum of problems in children who are referred to him and that the child referred cannot be assumed to be a child in need of both extensive evaluation and extensive psychotherapy. There is a range from those children with fairly well circumscribed problems that are readily delineated and for which little or no therapeutic intervention is required on up to a relatively small minority who are in need of more extensive diagnostic study and psychotherapy. In the vast majority for whom consultation is requested, he is likely to find that his more usual contribution is to help people delineate, understand, and resolve circumscribed problems over the course of no more than several sessions with them. The more a therapist appreciates this state of affairs, the more available he is likely to become.

Chances are also that if the therapist can make himself available with a more open-minded approach to problems, he may find himself more welcome. Many times those who refer and the families referred have felt frustrated because they have found child therapists to proceed in a stereotyped fashion that is not attuned to the needs of the patient but geared more to the needs of the therapist, be it to maintain ritualistic practices or theoretical biases. For example, in one setting a pediatrician commented, "We no longer refer patients to child psychiatry because we always hear the same story. Invariably, they say that this child is very much disturbed and ought to be referred to the local child guidance clinic. We don't need them to tell us that."

To sum it all up, child therapists need to avoid the pitfall of all those who espouse the establishment of rationality as their forte. Namely, they need watch that even as they espouse rationality, they themselves do not become irrational in their approaches. In a sense, the child psychotherapist prides himself in helping establish rationality in the quagmire of irrationality that so often engulfs children and families caught up in emotional problems. The more the child therapist succumbs to mythical assertions, ritualistic practices, and rationalized attitudes toward patients and their problems, the more he is likely to end up acting very irrationally. In a similar vein, the child psychotherapist needs to avoid becoming snared in his attempts to learn and to teach psychotherapy as though it were a "hard" science. If he needs to emphasize that psychotherapy is a science, fine, but then he ought to learn it and teach it as he would the science of music, writing, or even clinical medicine. It even seems possible that to the extent a therapist can approach therapy in this light and not get caught up in too deliberate an attempt to be completely scientific, the more reasonable and, if you will, the more scientific he can become.

REFERENCES

Adams, P. L., and McDonald, N. F.: Clinical cooling out of poor people. *Amer J Orthopsychiat, 38*:457, 1968.

Alexander, F.: In French, T. M., *et al.: Psychoanalytic Therapy.* New York, Ronald Press, 1946.

Allen, F. H.: *Psychotherapy with Children.* New York, Norton, 1942.

Ausubel, D. P.: *Theory and Problems of Child Development.* New York, Grune and Stratton, 1958.

Bateson, G. D., Jackson, D., Haley, J., and Weakland, J.: Toward a theory of schizophrenia. *Behav Sci, 1*:251, 1956.

Beres, D.: The effects of extreme deprivation in infancy on psychic structure in adolescence: A study in ego development. *Psychoanal Stud Child, 5*:212, 1950.

Bettelheim, B.: *The Children of the Dream.* Toronto, Macmillan, 1969.

Brody, S.: Aims and methods in child psychotherapy. *J Amer Acad Child Psychiat, 3*:385, 1964.

Buxbaum, E.: Technique of child therapy: A critical evaluation. *Psychoanal Stud Child, 9*:297, 1954.

Ekstein, R.: Expressed in a conference on psychotherapy, 1968.

Ekstein, R., and Friedman, S. W.: The function of acting out, play action and play acting in the psychotherapeutic process. *J Amer Psychoanal Ass, 5*:581, 1957.

Erikson, E. H.: *Childhood and Society.* New York, Norton, 1950.

Frank, Jerome D.: *Persuasion and Healing.* Baltimore, Johns Hopkins, 1961.

Freud, A.: Indications for child analysis. *Psychoanal Stud Child, 1*:127, 1945.

Freud, A.: *The Psychoanalytical Treatment of Children.* New York, International Universities Press, 1946.

Freud, A.: *Normality and Pathology in Childhood.* New York, International Universities Press, 1965.

Fries, M. E.: Some hypotheses on the role of the congenital activity type in personality development. *Psychoanal Stud Child, 8*:48, 1953.

Glover, E.: *The Technique of Psychoanalysis.* New York, International Universities Press, 1955.

Greenson, R. R.: *The Technique and Practice of Psychoanalysis.* New York, International Universities Press, 1967, vol. I.

Hambidge, G., Jr.: Structured play therapy. *Amer J Orthopsychiat, 25*:601, 1955.

Harrison, S. I., and Carek, D. J.: *Guide to Psychotherapy.* Boston, Little, Brown, 1966.

Hess, E. H.: Imprinting. *Science, 130*:133, 1959.

Hug-Hellmuth, H. V.: On the technique of child analysis. *Int J Psychoanal, 2*:287, 1921.

Jackson, D. D., and Weakland, J. H.: Conjoint family treatment. *Psychiatry, 24* (Suppl. 2):30, 1961.

Johnson, A. M.: Sanctions for superego lacunae of adolescents. In *Searchlights on Delinquency.* New York, International Universities Press, 1949.

Joselyn, I. M.: Child psychiatric clinics—Quo Vadimus?—*J Amer Acad Child Psychiat, 3*:721, 1964.

Klein, M.: *The Psychoanalysis of Children,* 3rd ed. London, Hogarth Press, 1959.

Lipton, E. L., Steinschneider, A., and Richmond, J. B.: Autonomic function in the neonate. IV. Individual differences in cardiac reactivity. *Psychosom Med, 23*:472, 1961.

Murphy, L. B.: *The Widening World of Childhood.* New York, Basic Books, 1962.

Nuffield, E. J. A.: Child psychiatry limited: A conservative viewpoint. *J Amer Acad Child Psychiat, 7*:210, 1968.

Panel Report. The relationship between child analysis and the theory and practice of adult psychoanalysis. *J Amer Psychoanal Ass, 13*:159, 1965.

Redl, F.: A strategy and techniques of the life space interview. *Amer J Orthopsychiat, 29*:1, 1959.

Sandler, A. M.: Inconsistency in the mother as a factor in character development: A comparative study of three cases. *Psychoanal Stud Child, 12*:209, 1957.

Singer, E.: *Key Concepts in Psychotherapy.* New York, Random House, 1965.

Spitz, R. A.: Hospitalism: An inquiry into the genesis of psychiatric conditions in early childhood. *Psychoanal Stud Child, 1*:53, 1945.

Sylvester, E., and Cooper, S.: Truisms and slogans in the practice and teaching of child psychotherapy. *J Amer Acad Child Psychiat, 5*:617, 1966.

Waelder, R.: The psychoanalytic theory of play. *Psychoanal Quart, 2*:208, 1933.

Watson, A. S.: The conjoint psychotherapy of marriage partners. *Amer J Orthopsychiat, 33*:912, 1963.

Whyte, L. L.: *The Unconscious Before Freud.* New York, Basic Books, 1960.

Wolff, P. H.: The causes, controls and organization of behavior in the neonate. *Psychol Issues, V*:1, Monogr. 17, 1966.

INDEX